Multisensory Landscape Design

A Designer's Guide for Seeing

Daniel Roehr

Cover image: Daniel Roehr

First published 2022
by Routledge
4 Park Square, Milton Park, Abingdon, Oxon OX14 4RN

and by Routledge
605 Third Avenue, New York, NY 10158

Routledge is an imprint of the Taylor & Francis Group, an informa business

© 2022 Daniel Roehr

The right of Daniel Roehr to be identified as author of this work has been asserted in accordance with sections 77 and 78 of the Copyright, Designs and Patents Act 1988.

All rights reserved. No part of this book may be reprinted or reproduced or utilised in any form or by any electronic, mechanical, or other means, now known or hereafter invented, including photocopying and recording, or in any information storage or retrieval system, without permission in writing from the publishers.

Trademark notice: Product or corporate names may be trademarks or registered trademarks, and are used only for identification and explanation without intent to infringe.

British Library Cataloguing-in-Publication Data
A catalogue record for this book is available from the British Library

Library of Congress Cataloging-in-Publication Data
Names: Roehr, Daniel, author.
Title: Multisensory landscape design : a designer's guide for seeing / Daniel Roehr.
Description: New York, NY : Routledge, 2022. | Includes bibliographical references and index. |
Identifiers: LCCN 2021053865 (print) | LCCN 2021053866 (ebook) | ISBN 9781138586796 (hardback) | ISBN 9781138586802 (paperback) | ISBN 9780429504389 (ebook)
Subjects: LCSH: Landscape design. | Senses and sensation. | Intersensory effects. | Design--Human factors.
Classification: LCC SB472.45 R66 2022 (print) | LCC SB472.45 (ebook) | DDC 712--dc23/eng/20211216
LC record available at https://lccn.loc.gov/2021053865
LC ebook record available at https://lccn.loc.gov/2021053866

ISBN: 9781138586796 (hbk)
ISBN: 9781138586802 (pbk)
ISBN: 9780429504389 (ebk)

DOI: 10.4324/9780429504389

Typeset in Futura
by Paratype

Printed in the UK by Severn, Gloucester on responsibly sourced paper

Publisher's Note
This book has been prepared from camera-ready copy provided by the author.

For Cornelia Hahn Oberlander,
who taught us to be persistent in our learning,
to be passionate about every endeavour we take on,
to listen with kindness and be polite,
and to remain patient and persevere,
no matter the odds.

Acknowledgments

A book is always a creation of many people. Foremost, I would like to wholeheartedly thank Michelle Gagnon-Creeley, without whom this book would not exist. It began with a directed study she did with me at UBC about hand sketching, which inspired the creation of a seminar on seeing not only through hand sketching but using all five senses. Michelle was instrumental in setting up the seminar, which culminated in writing this book, and supported it all the way as contributing author, editor, graphic designer, and motivator.

Second, I would like to thank the Seeing Environment classes of 2018 and 2020 for trying out the seminar exercises and the many who allowed their drawings to be used as examples for Chapter 4. I would especially like to thank the following students for their images: Jenna Ratzlaff, Valia Puente, Mingjia Chen, Kemeng Gao, Samantha Hart, Marissa Campbell, Fabian Lobmueller, Yaying Zhou, Wenwen Zhuang, Kathryn Pierre, Berend Kessler, Yette Gram, Vicky Cen, Jennifer Reid, Josh Fender, Jonathan Behnke, Jacob Darowski, and Doug Craig.

I would also like to thank Neda Rhoonia for creating the garden maps in Chapter 3, and Feiyu Wei for her research and translations on multisensorial gardens in China. A big thank you to Jordon Lypkie, Marissa Campbell, and Duncan Chambers for their insightful comments and rigorous edits of the book manuscript.

And finally, my partner Jane Green, who also kindly supported me in writing the book.

Contributors

Daniel Roehr, MBCSLA, CSLA, AKB. Author. Roehr is an Associate Professor at the University of British Columbia School of Architecture and Landscape Architecture in Vancouver, Canada. He is a registered landscape architect in British Columbia and Berlin as well as a horticulturalist. Daniel has earned a Higher National Diploma (HND) in Horticulture and Landscape Technology from Askham Bryan College (York, England) and a BA (Hons) in Landscape Architecture from Heriot-Watt University / Edinburgh College of Art (Edinburgh, Scotland).

He is the founder and director of greenskinslab at UBC. For nearly three decades, his research has focused on international living roof design, construction, and low impact development (LID) as part of holistic stormwater management. This work is documented in his co-authored book Living Roofs in Integrated Urban Water Systems (Routledge 2015). Since 2013, he has been exploring how to make the concepts of LID accessible and acceptable to the public through animated hand drawn videos.

In recent years Daniel's research has expanded into how to teach visual literacy and multisensorial literacy to students accustomed to using computers. Roehr is also interested in the role of architectural hand drawing as a research tool to see the environment and to guide design iterations, and he shares his drawings on Instagram.

He has practiced extensively in Europe, North America, and Asia. From 1995 to 2000, he was project architect of the ground-breaking water sensitive living roof design of the Daimler-Chrysler Green Roof Project, Potsdamer Platz, Berlin, Germany. In 2013 he was a UBC Sustainability Research Fellow and was selected as a team member to compete in designing the Canadian National Holocaust Memorial in Ottawa. In 2016 he received the Killam Teaching Prize from UBC.

https://blogs.ubc.ca/drawingsdanielroehr/
https://www.instagram.com/danielroehrdrawings/

Michelle Gagnon-Creeley, Contributing Author, Research and Graphics. Gagnon-Creeley is a landscape designer, writer, and artist based in Vancouver. She holds a master's degree in landscape architecture from the University of British Columbia, and a bachelor's degree in urban planning from Concordia University. Gagnon-Creeley's work critically examines landscape architecture with regard to mindfulness, design as storytelling, decolonization, Indigenous sovereignty, and racial justice.

Contents

Preface ... x

Chapter 1 ... 1
From Visual to Multisensorial Literacy

Chapter 2 ... 17
Multisensorial Design Thinking

Chapter 3 ... 59
Sensewalks

Chapter 4 ... 101
Becoming Multisensorial

Chapter 5 ... 209
Teaching Multisensorial Literacy

Chapter 6 ... 227
Conclusion

Glossary ... 233

Index ... 237

0.1
A landscape drawn by the author at the age of 13.

Preface

This is a textbook for design students, professionals, and educators that aims to teach visual literacy using the five senses: touch, sound, taste, smell, and sight. This book puts forward a plea for a shift in design education—design educators must begin to teach and practice multisensorial literacy and place-based mindfulness. It is essential that design curricula help establish designers who are capable of immersing in, and deeply understanding the spaces that they are designing.

Since childhood, art has been my second oxygen. Many of my ancestors were artists, reaching back generations. My father was an artist, and my mother was an art dealer. Art, and especially drawing, has been my anchor in life. Drawing was my language as a child. I did not really like realistic drawing at the time; I would copy the Dada artists and Bauhaus pupils that my mother exhibited. Realistic drawing meant rules and precise observation—I wanted to express how I felt or what I experienced. I was always a rebel, creating my own drawing methods and expressive styles. This gave me the ability to draw and experiment without apprehension from early on in life. When I was a child, my mother explained to me that before Picasso drew abstractly, he was trained to draw realistically. This had an impression on me. Later, while studying to become a landscape architect, I learned how to excel in drawing from my first-year lecturer, William "Bill" Tucker. Bill, a wonderfully gifted drawer, was my most influential mentor and one of my dearest friends until his sudden early death. His teaching also initiated my desire to follow in his footsteps to become a teacher myself.

Along with being an artist, my father also trained as an art teacher. He never praised my work—he knew that the work was above average for a five-year-old, but always responded with "do another one," encouraging me to continue to get better and learn to critique my own work. Drawing was a way to express ideas and thoughts just for myself; it was like my own visual secret language. In comparison with the strict regurgitative learning in Bavarian primary school, I could express my ideas through my own means of communication. This ability has guided me throughout my professional and academic career. I realized early on that I was a visual learner. I could remember whole cities and landscapes spatially, but I could not yet graphically represent them, as I had not learned techniques like perspectival drawing. Learning the English vocabulary was much harder for me. Many children do not know that they might be stronger visual learners, especially as typical Western pedagogy focuses on the repetition of facts, formulas, and text. Both skills are important, but often art is not seen as being on a par with math, science, and technology. After primary school, art is seen as an elective subject in many schools. The often-suppressed treatment of art in high school can have the negative impact of school children being less visually literate upon graduating compared to schools where art is seen as equal to the other subjects taught. Many students, especially coming from other undergraduate disciplines in the sciences, may feel under-equipped or incapable of producing visual material in professional graduate design programs.

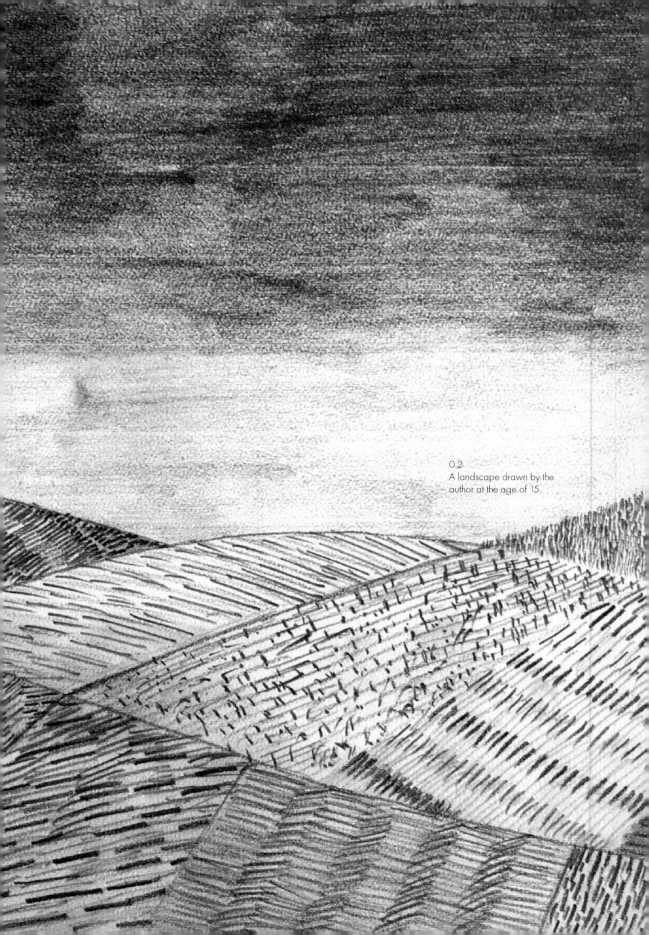

0.2
A landscape drawn by the author at the age of 15.

After secondary school I spent time training to be a gardener. It was during this time that one of my instructors noted a plan I had drawn for a garden bed and encouraged me to study landscape architecture—a profession I had heard of from my mother when digging a pond in our community courtyard garden at the age of 12. It was the content of my drawing which inspired the horticulture teacher to initiate my journey to become a landscape architect, but this experience also encouraged me to further develop my abstract drawing. Many drawing phases followed, but the most influential was during my three-year working period in Tokyo, Japan. Here I relied on drawing to communicate my ideas, making up for the gaps in my spoken Japanese. I devised a very fast sketch language and realized the immense power that drawing can hold as an international language and design thinking tool. Since this experience in the early 1990s I have kept all my sketches and archived them to document my learning process. I have used them in my lectures, and in March 2019 I launched @danielroehrdrawings on Instagram, and Off Screen Studio, a blog discussing my drawings. These tools show intentionally unedited drawings to give viewers, and especially students, an honest view into learning to draw. It is a skill-developing process, which is imperfect by nature. I also use these tools to demonstrate the role that drawing plays in design thinking and processes.

Computer technology in the last century has had profound effects on society and has shifted the way that humans think and function. In the context of landscape architecture and architecture, technology has caused a major shift in the way that designers analyze and conceptualize—hand drawing no longer plays the same role that it once did in a student's design process. While technological knowledge is important to foster in design pedagogy, it is also essential to strike a balance between the computer and the hand. Students should also be learning critical thinking, communication, collaboration, and creativity. Visual literacy can embrace these four skills in design teaching. This book proposes a framework of observation tools, design strategies, and exercises for how visual literacy could be inserted into contemporary design pedagogy.

The book suggests expanding on existing theories about developing visual literacy to include the five main senses, referring to this practice as multisensorial literacy. It encourages a new method of design that allows for place-based mindfulness with consideration of all of the senses and provides examples of how multisensorial thinking can create more inclusive designs. The book also delves into each of the five senses and their relevance to design, providing exercises to encourage seeing and observation. The book is divided into six chapters— each beginning with theory and ending with tangible exercises and examples that can be practiced. Each chapter has recommended readings that were inspirational throughout the writing of the book and could be enriching to those looking to delve deeper into visual and multisensorial literacy. The proposed exercises can either be done by hand drawing, digital drawing, or a combination of techniques and media. The book concludes with a list of recommendations for integrating multisensorial teaching in design education and provides suggestions for future research. It is hoped that this book will be a good resource for students, teachers, and readers interested in multisensorial design. Thank you for taking the time to embark on this journey of discovery.

Chapter 1

From Visual to Multisensorial Literacy

A Redefinition of Seeing

The ways one moves and interacts in space are inherent considerations in spatial design. When first learning about spatial design, it is imperative that students begin to understand the spatial experience. Visual literacy and multisensorial literacy are key to deeply understanding spatial design, and the advent of digital technology in design disciplines has led to a de-emphasis in the teaching of these skills in current design pedagogy. Technology has been immensely powerful in the ways that designers can analyze and represent the world, but it has also arguably numbed us from using our bodies and senses to design. While we recognize the importance of digital technology to designers today, we are calling for new and seasoned designers to learn to be physically present again—to let our bodies be the recording devices. We are also calling for a renewed definition of seeing, one which encompasses all of the senses—not just the visual.

Why is it that we have become singularly focused on the visual? Sight has dominated the hierarchy of the senses in Western thought since ancient Greece, where philosophers elevated it as the highest sense. Greek architecture was designed for the "pleasure of the eye" (Pallasmaa, 2005, p. 26). This train of thought continued throughout the Renaissance, when the five senses were ranked, with vision being the paramount sense and touch considered of "least importance" (Pallasmaa, 2005, p. 15). The invention of linear perspective drawing during the Renaissance made the eye the "center point of the perceptual world" (Pallasmaa, 2005, p. 16). Prior to the Renaissance, the architect was heavily involved in a project from its conception to its construction. This practice shifted during this period, when a separation was made possible between the drawing and the construction, allowing "for more abstract thought and experimentation, as clearly risks are straightforward on paper" (Biddulph, 2014, p. 282). The constructed visual representation of art and architecture during the Renaissance enforced the dominance of sight over the other senses. The observer was viewing intricately constructed images, but not feeling them—there was no reference to, or space for, the other senses. We are still heavily influenced by the eye today—as our entire world is essentially mediated by screens—in advertisements, maps, and the printed word. We are completely immersed in the visual. Our other senses continue to play a more subconscious and inhibited role in the Western world, with some exceptions.

1.1
Gestural drawings, drawn by the author, 2019

A child first learns to "see" through touch before using their eyes, oftentimes grabbing and placing a new object in their mouth to experience how it feels. They learn to "see" visual images later on, and later still can begin to synthesize and express these sensory feelings. The art critic John Berger wrote "seeing comes before words, the child recognizes before it can speak" (1972, p. 7). Our bodies are vessels that hold immense power to perceive and engage with the world in a myriad of ways. They have the capacity to physically store emotions and memories, and vividly connect us to space through many senses if we are mindful enough to allow for it. It is for these reasons that seeing should be re-framed as a multisensorial experience. Our bodies should be treated as the first recording device of our design process. The architect Juhani Pallasmaa wrote "every touching experience of architecture is multi-sensory; qualities of space, matter and scale are measured equally by the eye, ear, nose, skin, tongue, skeleton and muscle" (2005, p. 41). A well-designed space will engage with all of the senses—but how can we do that when we are taught only to see with our eyes?

After the multisensorial experience comes perception, which is the conscious outcome of this experience. Many designers, scientists, and scholars have written on seeing and perception, and it becomes apparent that it is not the act of sight alone which makes us physically perceive the world, but a holistic multisensorial process. In Christopher Tilley and Wayne Bennett's book *Body and Image*, the authors note how perception "is a recording of sensations brought about by objects that are external to the mind" (2008, p. 22). Perception also has an element of memory and emotion to it—as our bodies engage with a space, our minds are recalling memories and sensations (Tilley & Bennett, 2008, p. 22; Swailes, 2016, p. 23). All acts of perception are deeply personal, as they involve our corporeal experience. With our perceptions and memories come emotions (Swailes, 2016, p. 34). For example, the experience of certain smells on a site can affect us emotionally, recalling a past memory of the same smell during a happy or sad time.

Thus, seeing is not only the sight of the visual image, or a "retinal journey" as Pallasmaa describes it (2005, p. 12). Seeing is a corporeal, multisensorial experience that embodies the sensation of the present environment, combined with memories of previously experienced sounds, smells, touch, tastes, and visuals. Seeing is a complex and holistic bodily experience and should be acknowledged as such in design practice and education.

1.2
Memory drawing of the
Okanagan Valley, Canada,
drawn by the author, 2019

The Importance of Seeing for Designers

Seeing the environment and understanding our perceptions of it are important in the design process. It is the foundation of designing, and it can be learned and practiced. But as suggested above, the visual experience should not be the only consideration. All five senses should create a holistic multisensorial experience and process of perception for designing.

Juhani Pallasmaa has been an advocate for understanding multisensorial perception in teaching and practicing architectural design throughout his extensive professional and academic career. He recognizes that as designers our body and mind are at the forefront of how we design— our senses piece together a framework to understand the world. Our relationship with the world cannot be removed from how we design spaces. Good design "integrates physical and mental structures" (Pallasmaa, 2015, p. 12). It is important for us as designers to recognize that our bodies, and in particular our senses, are recording mechanisms that can help guide us as we absorb and create. Therefore, it is important that educators develop more opportunities to practice this mindfulness in design education.

Doing fieldwork has not only been on the decline in design, but also in other disciplines such as archeology and anthropology "due to [expanded possibilities for] desk work and remotely gathered and interpreted information" (Swailes, 2016, p. 24). At the time of writing this book, during a global pandemic, this dynamic has increasingly become the norm. Photography and video have become the visual observation and recording tools in the field for landscape architecture, architecture, and urban design, "shifting the field emphasis from analytical sketching to visual survey" (Swailes, 2016, p. 24). What is missing is the bodily experience; the conscious engagement of the five senses. Being in the field initiates a wider range of sensations apart from visuals, and "a multisensorial experience informs perception" (Swailes, 2016, p. 34).

Site immersion consciously uses all the senses to engage deeply with a site. This could include spending extensive periods of time observing and listening to the sounds of different birds to determine if the site is ecologically healthy, or analyzing the smells of a specific area and their source to determine if the site is pleasant to use. Remote observation often misses out on the personal perception and emotional interpretation of a site. Field experience and notation (visual notes diagrammed or drawn, written, photographed, or sound and video recorded) initiates a deliberate thinking process on site and when processing recorded information at the desk (Swailes, 2016, p. 37). Site immersion in the environment, writes Swailes, "is inevitably accompanied by factors we cannot predict, and it is this engagement with chance, as well as degrees of control, that makes fieldwork a good proxy for the lived landscape experience of others" (Swailes, 2016, p. 35). Site immersion is multisensorial and initiates unforeseen sensations, experiences, and emotions, leading to a holistic site understanding.

Visiting a project site and its context regularly before and during the design process is important; with every visit new experiences, sensations, and conditions will be discovered. Those discoveries might change the initial perception of the site and alter the problem-solving strategies during the design process. Site immersion is part of the design process—allowing for early design thoughts to form immediately or be picked up later. Chapter 5 describes in detail why this is important when teaching design studios.

Teaching Seeing in Today's Context

When learning to design for the environment, students need to gradually understand the spatial experience—how to move through, interact with, and read space—from small to large scale. The ability to read space is paramount in early design education. In contemporary design pedagogy, we teach this skill through visual literacy, where students are taught to see the world around them and to understand, analyze, and interpret these observations visually. The visual meaning is normally recorded by referential and analytical annotated sketches and drawings (see Chapter 3), diagrams, collages, and cardboard models. However, in the packed syllabi of design programs today, multisensorial literacy—especially through hand drawing, is on the decline.

This book suggests an all-senses, inclusive, pedagogical point of view acknowledging that sight has historically been the main sensory focus in design teaching. Past research and publications on visual literacy in design focus mainly on referring to what we see before us, recording it through drawing and visual note taking. Designers have established definitions for visual, but not for multisensorial literacy. In *Visual Notes for Architects and Designers*, Norman Crowe and Paul Laseau view visual literacy as both "visual acuity and visual expression" where "visual acuity is an intense ability to see information or multiple messages in one's environment with clarity and accuracy" and "visual expression is the ability to initiate visual messages" (2012, p. 7). The ability to see information or multiple messages includes hearing, tasting, smelling, and touching, but this has not explicitly been taught in design education nor has it been addressed in their book. Catherine Dee's influential *Form and Fabric in Landscape Architecture* is one of the first books in landscape architecture which expands its focus beyond sight alone. Dee acknowledges what others take for granted; that "we tend to underestimate the strength of influences of other senses on our experience of landscape" (Dee, 2001, p. 191). She suggests that "the senses together enable us to make sense of place" (Dee, 2001, p. 191). Despite these observations being made about the predominance that the visual holds, design education continues to focus on sight (Have & van den Toorn, 2012, p. 74). In this book, we suggest removing this hierarchical thinking and paying equal attention to each of the main senses while recording and analyzing a site. This strategy will reduce visual presumptions and treat every design problem as a lived experience and not just a series of visual compositions.

Exploring the use of hand drawing to develop visual literacy is no longer emphasized in design schools in the same way that it was during the times of the Bauhaus or the École des Beaux Arts. Current theory has developed two reasons for why this is: 1) hand drawing and visual literacy are both skills that are now treated as "innate skill" (Moore, 2003, p. 34), and 2) the advent of new technology has led students and educators to emphasize the learning of new software over learning more conventional modes of design like hand drawing, and many design programs have shifted their curriculum to accommodate for that.

Design instructors perceive visual literacy as something that students are expected to have before entering the design world. This belief has created a system in which new design thinkers can be overwhelmed when attempting to teach themselves a skill that is no longer extensively taught in the architectural curriculum. The ability to draw has been seen by designers in tandem with visual literacy, and with it the notion that a student inherently knows how to draw prior to even entering a design program. While sketching will take place in some of the earlier courses in a design program sequence, sketching has ultimately become "separated from normal architectural discourse" (Jenkins, 2013, p. 29) due to the introduction of new technology. This can be daunting for students who are coming from backgrounds that are not in the fine arts and have not been taught about hand drawing or visual analysis. Furthermore, in a society where failure and taking risks is perceived as negative, students are often afraid to learn through media with which they are unfamiliar (Adams, 1986, p. 44). As Brumberger notes, "students often come to our classes with the firm belief that they have no talent and therefore cannot learn to be good visual communicators. This belief stands in the way of their learning to think visually, which in turn stands in the way of their learning to communicate visually" (2007, p. 383).

The Hand vs. The Computer

Technology has caused a major shift in the way that designers analyze and conceptualize—hand drawing no longer plays the same role that it once did in a student's design process. While technological knowledge is important to foster in design pedagogy, it is important to strike a balance between the computer and the hand. As Treib notes "electronic processing does not yet substitute for thinking" (2008, p. viii). Northcut and Brumberger conducted a study regarding the influence of technology in education and its effect on students. The results indicated that the emphasis on technology in design education "undermine[d] that learning process" (Northcut & Brumberger, 2010, p. 463). It was observed that students were spending most of their time "creating effects with technology" rather than learning about the design process (Northcut & Brumberger, 2010, p. 464). This pointed to a larger issue of students neglecting important aspects of their design process, such as engaging with the site or developing a strong design concept, in favour of developing their graphic and technological skills. The use of the camera, AutoCAD, and Google Maps are note-worthy examples of technology that can be extremely useful but also potentially detrimental to the learning process in early design education.

For instance, the camera serves as an excellent tool for capturing a site quickly and is a useful memory/recording and thinking tool in site analysis (and we will touch on this more in Chapter 3). There is also cause to be wary about using cameras before practicing site immersion, as photographs "cannot record concepts, underlying structure, schematic organization, or anything else that the eye cannot see all at once" (Crowe & Laseau, 2012, p. 1). Crowe and Laseau argue that the camera has led to a "decline in visual literacy in general" (2012, p. 1). The speed and ease of photography does not convey the emotions or atmosphere of a space, both of which are crucial to site analysis. The same can be said about mapping applications such as Google Maps. While these applications are integral for developing an understanding of the site, they do not convey how all the senses are being stimulated and the perception that the viewer has when physically present on the site. This is where sketching provides something that the camera cannot capture. Sketching in-situ allows students to develop "a personal response to the locality" (Hutchinson, 2011, p. 11). On-site sketching forces one to spend more time in a place, walking and looking more closely, and perhaps noticing more quantifiable data in addition to a deeper qualitative or emotional understanding.

John May refers to the present state of design practice as the "post-orthographic period," where the output is not "a representation of the world" but "a presentation of the world—an automatic and perceptually up to date, real-time model of the world" (2017, p. 19). Technology has allowed us to produce images so fast that the perception and meaning of the changes can barely be processed by the brain fast enough. By using the computer, students

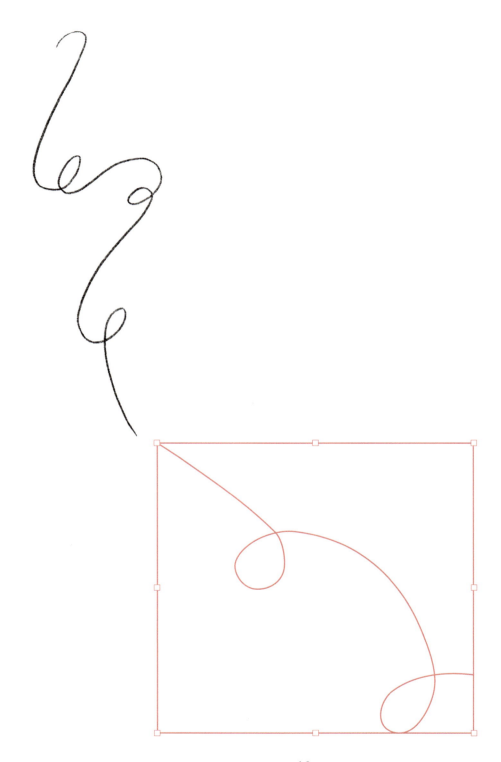

1.3
Lines drawn on a computer provide a much different character than lines drawn by hand; drawn by Michelle Gagnon-Creeley, 2020

are continuously processing images, leaving little space for drawing which May defines as a series of hand-mechanical gestures that can be learned through practice (May, 2017, p. 19).

However, like learning computer-based skills, drawing is a pedagogical learning tool. Drawing teaches seeing. Because it involves physically creating, it is a craft and a thinking tool. In fact, it is a multisensorial experience to draw, as it involves the senses of touch (hand/brain), sight (eye/brain), and sound (ear/brain). Hand sketching is an extremely fast visual communication tool that can also serve as an excellent learning and correction tool. If practiced regularly, one can produce immense numbers of recorded observations and perceptions experienced in the environment and analyze the problems visually through drawings. The fundamental purpose is to understand the meaning and produce an interpretation of the environmental context in relation to the design problem through drawing. Visual literacy means that hand drawing is not used just to record what one sees but to speculate beyond what is before us. Visual literary is the "interaction between knowing and seeing" (Bruno Latour as quoted in Have & van den Toorn, 2012, p. 74).

It is important to note that we are not making the case for abolishing technology in design. We recognize the vital importance that technology holds throughout the design process and that it has greatly improved the discipline. What we are calling for is equilibrium between learning technological skills and analog skills. We are calling for a hybrid in design pedagogy where both digital rendering and hand drawing can co-exist and complement one another.

With the constant visual distractions of the technological world around us, educators and students need to learn to see, interpret, and use visual imagery wisely in their design work and allow thinking time and physical space away from digital tools to see and experience the world. Human observation and recording skills have been extended with fast digital recording tools. Has the brain evolved at the same pace as the digital tools in the last decade? More research will be needed on this topic in the future. The digital tools are here to stay for the time being and should be used together with analog tools as a hybrid during analysis and the early design phase. While digital tools should be used in the later design and communication phase of the project, hand drawing should continue to be encouraged during the ideation and conceptualization process.

There should also be a shift in design education to allow for more site immersion. Syllabi throughout design education should include local studio projects that allow for regular site visits. During such visits, the different phases in design can be reiterated; seeing and multisensorial perception, analysis, thinking, and designing. In design syllabi there is often an imbalance of studio time to site time. Effective teaching and practicing of seeing can be better achieved by intensive site immersion (which we will discuss in Chapter 5).

1.4
The landscape as multisensorial, drawn by the author, 2020

Multisensorial Literacy as Solution

Multisensorial literacy involves intentionally seeing the world around us using the five senses to observe, understand, analyze, and interpret this information into something visual. Seeing and understanding the meaning of all senses within the environment, in combination with recording and interpreting it, and then communicating design ideas are the most important skills to be taught in design education. While the predominance of the visual has created inspiring architecture, the lack of inclusion of the other senses creates spaces that are impossible for everyone to connect to. Multisensorial design has the opportunity to fill this gap, and to create spaces that better integrate into the world around us.

As mentioned above, visual literacy is something that design teachers are far more familiar with teaching than multisensorial literacy. In multisensorial literacy, the observer has to record, perceive, and interpret the meanings of not only sight but of sound, touch, smell, and taste into visual imagery. Deeper explanations about all five senses are given in Chapter 4 along with exercises. These exercises explore techniques and methods for how those senses can be recorded with videos, collages, texts, performances, podcasts, annotated sketches, diagrams, and drawings. Drawing and sketching are placed first as they are also faster and more easily practiced in the field—so they also form the basis for the other media listed.

It is important to note that multisensorial perception skills are not the same as multisensorial literacy skills. Multisensorial perception skills are the conscious understanding and recording of the senses interplay with each other, for example sound and touch, or smell and taste, or sight and taste. Multisensorial literacy is the method to observe the context of the design problem with the five senses to understand, analyze, and document it through drawing and recording tools.

In Chapter 2 sensory recording and visualization tools for each sense are listed. And later on, those recordings and visualizations of the sensorial perception of the environment are interpreted and analyzed by combining them for a given design problem, such as the combination of smell and taste. The interpretation of the perceptional meaning of the senses can be practiced with exercises described in Chapter 4 that focus on each individual sense.

When teaching and practicing seeing in the design process, digital tools are indeed important, as they can initiate additional multisensorial observation and perception. Concrete interpretations can be drawn from all five senses through the practice of multisensorial observation and recording, combined with digital tools. Easily accessible digital tools can be used to interpret the meaning of multisensorial images, experiences, and sensations around us. For instance, the tablet can be used to draw images, and record sound or movement through video. These digital tools expand static visual image recording, thereby increasing the complexity of learning through seeing.

Recommended Reads

The Eyes of the Skin, Juhani Pallasmaa (2005)
This book focuses on the "Question of Perception" in architecture and how the senses hold significance in how humans experience architecture. It argues that the tactile (suppressed) senses are as important as, if not more important than, vision when designing. This book provides an understanding of why observation and perception with all the senses is important in the design process.

Drawn to Design, Eric Jenkins (2013)
This book is an essential tool for developing freehand analytical sketching skills in architecture. It has a succinct theoretical component explaining sketching as a method of exploration and design thinking. It acknowledges and includes digital design process and emphasizes freehand drawing as a recording and observation tool of the design environment. This book is important, as it provides a theoretical and visual argument including drawings as examples for why we need to continue to teach analytical hand drawing.

Form and Fabric in Landscape Architecture: A Visual Introduction, Catherine Dee (2001)
This book focuses on visual observation and perception, and analytical understanding of the environment to initiate design thinking. In the final chapters, Dee visualizes through drawings and text her own observations and personal (tacit) knowledge on the senses—how plants, structures, and rocks might smell, taste or feel—further developing this idea that site analysis can be a deeply personal experience. This book provides a comprehensive visual approach to the study of landscape architecture by creating a spatial morphology based on use and experience of landscapes.

Field Sketching and the Experience of Landscape, Janet Swailes (2016)
This book focuses on observing and recording the landscape through site immersion and field sketching. Primarily geared towards landscape architects, it is also applicable for architects and urban designers. The book has a theoretical component about field observation and perception and provides techniques and examples to practice field sketching. This book is a comprehensive textbook for how to sketch in the environment.

Drawing/Thinking-Confronting an Electronic Age, Marc Treib (Ed.) (2008)
This book is written by architects, landscape architects, artists, historians, and curators about their personal stories on the merits of hand drawing supporting the design process in the computer age. This book is important because it captures a specific time period in which many people trained in traditional design methods were trying to make sense of and confront the advent of electronic drawings and what it meant for teaching and practice.

Drawing for Landscape Architecture, Edward Hutchinson (2011)
This book combines traditional hand drawing techniques with CAD rendering. It is a textbook which guides readers from a site visit's first visual notes to concept, design ideas, and representation, as well as construction and site drawings. This book is important as it combines the use of analog and digital design processes.

References

Adams, J. (1986). *Conceptual Blockbusting: A Guide to Better Ideas.* Cambridge MA: Perseus Books.

Berger, J. (1972). *Ways of Seeing.* London, UK: Penguin Books.

Biddulph, M. (2014). Drawing and thinking: Representing place in the practice of place-making. *Journal of Urban Design, 19*(3), 287-297. doi:10.1080/13574809.2014.890045.

Brumberger, E. R. (2007). Making the strange familiar: A pedagogical exploration of visual thinking. *Journal of Business and Technical Communication, 21*(4), 376-401. doi: 10.1177/1050651907304021

Crowe, N. & Laseau, P. (2012). *Visual Notes for Architects and Designers.* Hoboken, NJ: John Wiley & Sons.

Dee, C. (2001). *Form and Fabric in Landscape Architecture: A Visual Introduction.* New York, NY: Routledge.

Have, R. & van der Toorn, M. (2012). The role of hand drawing in basic design education in the digital age, *ENMA 2012, 72*-80.

Hutchinson, E. (2011). *Drawing for Landscape Architecture.* New York, NY: Thames & Hudson.

Jasper, A., & Wagner, N. (2018). Smell E. Lupton and A. Lipps (Eds.) The Senses: Design beyond Vision (p. 50). New York, NY: Princeton Architecture Press.

Jenkins, E. J. (2013). *Drawn to Design.* Basel: Birkhauser.

May, J. (2017). Everything is already an image. *Log, 40,* 9-26. https://www.anycorp.com/store/log40

Moore, K. (2003). Overlooking the visual. *The Journal of Architecture, 8*(1), 24-50. doi:10.1080/1360236032000068497

Northcut, K. M. & Brumberger, E. R. (2010). Resisting the lure of technology-driven design: Pedagogical approaches to visual communication. *Technical Writing and Communication, 40*(4): 459-471. doi: 10.2190/TW.40.4.f

Pallasmaa, J. (2005). *The Eyes of the Skin.* Chichester: Wiley Publishing.

Swailes, J. (2016). *Field Sketching and the Experience of Landscape.* Abingdon, UK: Routledge.

Tilley, C. & Bennett, W. (2008). *Body and Image: Exploration in Landscape Phenomenology 2.* Walnut Creek, CA: Left Coast Press.

Treib, M. (2008). *Drawing/Thinking: Confronting an Electronic Age.* New York, NY: Routledge.

Chapter 2

Multisensorial Design Thinking

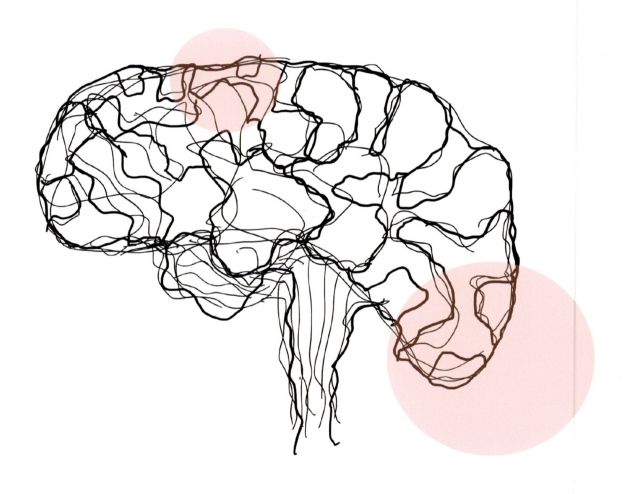

2.1
The human brain, drawn by the author, 2020

An Introduction to Multisensorial Literacy

This chapter provides a series of frameworks and checklists that can begin to break down what it means to develop multisensorial literacy. These tools support a more inclusive understanding of how to observe and perceive the five main senses (touch, sound, smell, taste, and sight), as well as initiate a more inclusive ideation process by involving all the senses. The proposed design process suggests formulating a priority list of the senses at the beginning and developing a matrix to decide which to include in the initial design vision. If the five senses are intentionally included in the design process from the beginning, more attention is paid to inclusive design outcomes.

Designing is communicating ideas. The word idea comes from the Greek word *idein*, which means "to see". How we record what we see can be done and represented in different ways. How we see and work on the design problem at hand can also be done in different ways. For designers, site immersion is paramount. Before we start to design, we need to see, understand, and record the existing conditions of the environment we are going to design for—from an object to a geographic region.

When observing a site through a multisensorial spatial experience, all senses should always be included throughout the analysis phase. A multisensorial observation will result in a more inclusive survey of the space and will help guide a mindful design. In the design phase however, not all senses will necessarily be included, as certain senses may be more applicable to the design than others.

The senses help:

- to order design priorities
- to define the design purpose
- to refine the built spatial experience
- to prioritize and synthesize the design purpose
- to perceive the design problem for each sense (touch, smell, taste, sound, sight)
- to refine the design problem
- to visualize the design problem with sound, movement, sight
- to invoke our memories and personal knowledge
- to create inclusive and personable spaces
- to understand and consider of the perspectives of people, for instance who are visual, hearing, or physically impaired in a society that privileges vision

When designing a small urban public garden there are many things to consider while first analyzing the site. We would want to understand its context within its specific location in a neighbourhood—how the surrounding position of buildings might cast shade on the garden, impacting the choice of appropriate plants to be included. We would want to examine the space in terms of accessibility—how the garden can be made wheelchair accessible from the street. These are considerations that we may be able to deduce from satellite imagery or online photos, but it would be much more enriching to personally visit the place in question. When we employ a site immersive, multisensorial strategy, the resulting analysis connects the body and mind to the place. For instance, recognizing the feeling of how your feet interact with the paved textured surface (smooth vs. rough vs. gritty) is as important as how the path looks and acts as a visual guide (colour, texture, visibility). With careful attention to the senses, we can better understand how others may interact with the place differently from their own default experience. For instance, the rolling vibration and sound of a wheelchair on this surface, or the ease of use for a person using a wheelchair could not be understood from photos alone.

2.2
A garden is a multisensorial space activating all the senses., drawn by the author, 2020

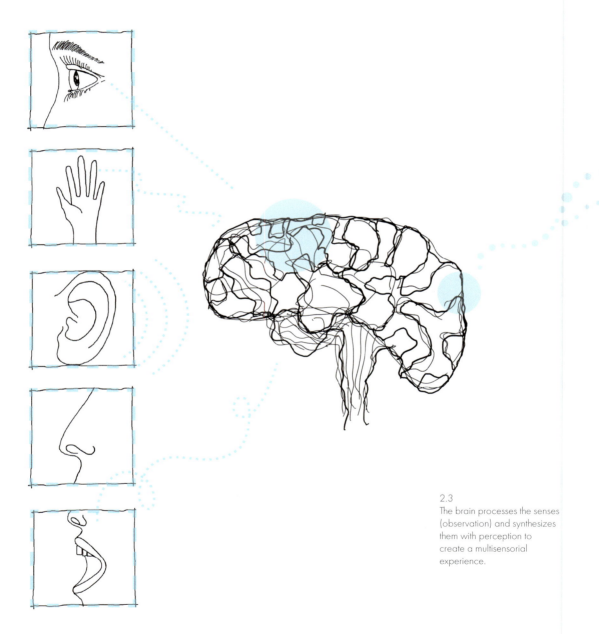

2.3
The brain processes the senses (observation) and synthesizes them with perception to create a multisensorial experience.

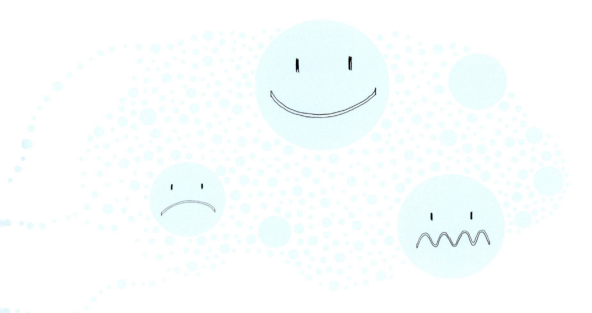

Observation vs. Perception

It is important to include all the senses when observing the context of a design problem and when designing the vision (Have & van den Toorn, 2012, p. 75). It is also important to distinguish between:

      a) observing : the cognitive act of hearing, tasting, touching, smelling, and seeing

      b) perception: the synthesis, memories, emotions, and feelings experienced in tandem with these new sensorial experiences

The observation and perception of the senses is complex and requires us to be extremely mindful in the ways that we interact with space. It is a challenge to rely solely upon our eyes to tell a story, but a dependence on sight alone provides us with an incomplete experience. The other senses should also be intentionally experienced, integrated, and documented, to more thoroughly understand the existing context in which one designs. Juhani Pallasmaa writes "an architectural work is not experienced as a series of isolated retinal pictures, but in its fully integrated material, embodied and spiritual essence" (Pallasmaa, 2005, p. 12).

An Overview of the Senses

We would be remiss without spending some time briefly defining these five senses that we keep mentioning and how they pertain to design in this book. A more detailed focus on each sense and how to record and render them can be found in Chapter 4.

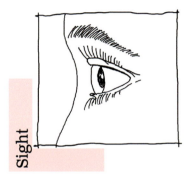

Sight is the translator of light and colour in our everyday life. Seeing gives us knowledge. The major problem in visual perception is what people see is not simply a translation of an image on the retina. We see the world right side up, even though the image on the retina is upside down (because it has passed through the lens). It is actually a much more complicated process that happens in order to create what we actually see. The key is that the brain works on the data from the eyes, and marries it with memories and guesses, all at lightning speed. The result is an experience of the world which looks to each person as if it were simple reality. However, although based on reality, it is actually a mental construct, built by the brain.

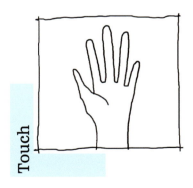

Touch is the first sense we experience and acquire (Mau, 2018, p. 22). Touch connects us, physically and spatially (three dimensionally) to the world. Pressure, temperature, light touch, vibration, pain, and other sensations are all part of the act of touching and are all attributed to different receptors in the skin. Touch is not only a functional necessity—it is important for human emotional well-being. Touch can influence our human perception, actions, and bodily awareness (Bradford, 2017). Touch is essential in design—it dictates the feeling of an object, and how our bodies move and physically interact within a space.

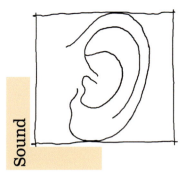

Sound

Sound in its most scientific form is a chain of molecules that vibrate in a wave that is initiated by a source of disturbance (Lupton, 2018, p. 44). When the wave hits the inner ear, the vibration causes the brain to process the wave as what we refer to as sound (Lupton, 2018, p. 44). Sound is a spatial experience; it is physical, as the vibrations provide a sensorial experience that can feel open or enclosed depending on the materiality and design of the space. For example, animals like whales and bats use echolocation to visualize their world.

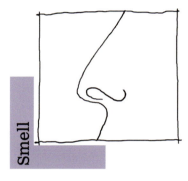

Smell

Research on smell has been minimal, but in recent years we have learned a great deal about how our noses work. New research suggests that humans can discriminate among one trillion different odours (Jasper & Wagner, 2018, p. 50; Lipps, 2018, p. 121). Smell is memory (Lipps, 2018, p. 110). Smell is spatial. For example, Japanese bathrooms made with cedar wood do not only have antiseptic properties, but the citrus scent also creates a clean atmosphere (Lipps, 2018, p. 113). Smell is everywhere and the information it carries is important for survival and pleasure (Lipps, 2018, p. 110).

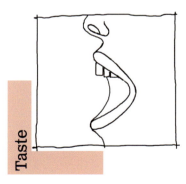

Taste

On the tongue there are little bumps called taste buds which have the ability to differentiate five tastes: sweet, salty, sour, bitter, and umami. Our tongues can also experience a sensation/perception of temperature, such as the heat from a hot pepper or the cooling effect of mint (Patterson & Aftel, 2017, p. 27). We would be remiss if we did not mention the leading role that the nose plays in all of this (with the mouth playing more of a supporting role). When we combine smell with taste, we get flavour, which is where things start to get interesting. Flavour is not just how the food tastes on your tongue; it is a combination of smell, texture, and visual appearance. It is a deeply personal sense; not one person shares the exact same preferences. Flavour perception changes over time as we grow older and our taste buds lose their sensitivity, and we begin to prefer the taste of coffee over candy. Taste is like a musical composition using all of the other senses to create the symphony of flavours that makes up the tasting experience.

The Phases of Design

Design is a series of events that begin with a site visit and end with a built space, including its maintenance, growth, and development over time.

There are generally six phases of design:

       1) Site immersion
       2) Recording
       3) Analysis
       4) Synthesis
       5) Ideation
       6) Final design

This process is not necessarily linear, and often takes on a circular movement or flux between phases.

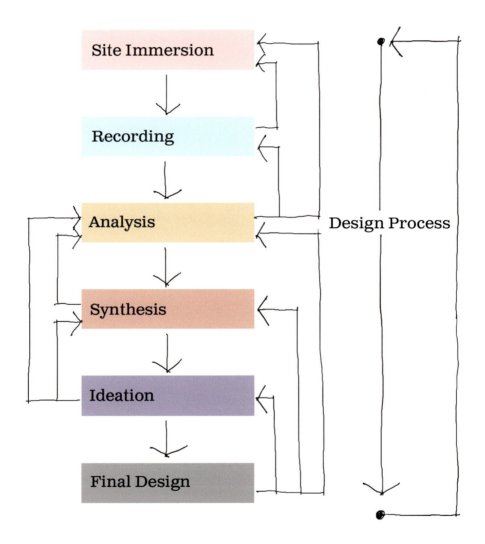

2.4
The design process.

2.5
Site Immersion

1) Site Immersion

To observe and understand the space for which you are designing, physically visiting and immersing within it is crucial. Site immersion is the first physical engagement with the site, and this procedure should be repeated multiple times throughout the entire design process. As design is a continuously changing operation, the site must be understood from many different angles. Site analysis is best achieved by roaming, as it provides the most comprehensive observation and perception of the site. If a site is too large to walk and a car or plane is used, the observation becomes solely visual. To achieve a holistic multisensorial site understanding, multiple walking excursions should be carried out to achieve a holistic, multisensorial site understanding.

2) Recording

There are multiple tools available to record the observations, perceptions, and sensations experienced during site immersion. A list of tools is provided later in this chapter, in the Multisensorial Perception Recording and Visualization Tools table. Traditionally, field sketching, photography, writing, and maps were used. These tools have typically been used to document visual observations, often ignoring the other senses. Today, with easier access to digital tools, we can also record sound, movement, and even temperature. This allows for a wider multisensorial palette of recording. Recording is a thinking process that has been traditionally done by hand drawing with annotation. With digital sound recording tools we can record the sounds we hear. The action of visually and digitally recording the observations, perceptions, and sensations of the site immersion experience ignites the design thinking process. Chapter 4 shows examples of multisensorial recording.

2.6
Recording

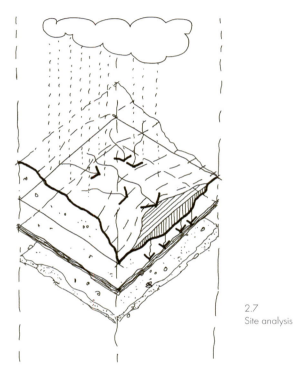

2.7
Site analysis

3) Analysis

Site analysis is the process of creating an inventory of everything that has been recorded, and then developing theories, conclusions, and ideas. The analysis primarily deals with revealing the information of a site that is not visible to the eye, as it relates to the site and its surrounding context. Traditionally, hand drawings, maps, and diagrams were used to carry out the analysis in design. Plan, section, elevation, perspective views, and block diagrams, oblique and exploded views were all used to reveal the visible and invisible. Today a combination of digital modelling and hand drawing are used to carry out the analysis. The analysis begins the detailed design process by exposing the visual and non-visual data of a site, creating initial design ideas. This type of synthesis is described in more detail in Chapter 4.

4) Synthesis

Synthesis is the process of bringing together all the data from the site analysis and the design program (design wishes by the client) and determining through drawing how to approach design problems and generate ideas to address the design program. The drawing tools include mapping, diagrams, orthographic drawings, and layering of drawings and perspectives "to visualize processes, sequences and change" (Have & van den Toorn, 2012, p. 76). The drawing tools are used to visualize the combined thoughts of the analysis and initiate design ideas. This process is a cycle in continuous flux and repeatedly raises new analytical observations and design questions until the designer is satisfied with the result. This part of the drawing process "takes place in the mind and results in a visual representation, a drawing, a sketch," or digital modelling (Have & van den Toorn, 2012, p. 76). The synthesis is a combination of the client's wishes, the program, and the analysis, visualized through drawn ideas.

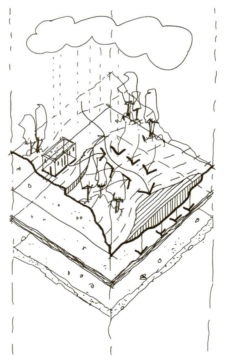

2.8
Synthesis

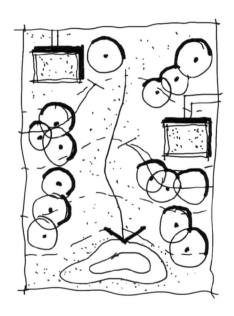

2.9
Ideation

5) Ideation

The ideation process is the imagination of what a site could be. This is a process where a range of design proposals is drawn for a site to test the possibilities of different ideas. The drawings act as a representational, thinking, and decision-making tool. Ideas are refined through different drawing scales, ultimately supporting the decision for the final design proposal. The design ideas should offer different answers to the problems at hand. Many designs, however, can create new problems, requiring new design solutions. It is therefore important to always consider alternative approaches to the design problem.

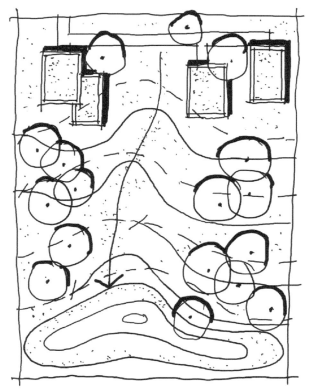

2.10
Final Design

6) Final Design

The final design is a set of drawn ideas with orthographic drawings, including digital 3D and physical models, diagrams, perspectives, and recently, animated 3D videos with sound. The final design also presents, in more detail, the concept of the project, and uses detailed drawings to explain it: for example, how the structure of the building would look or how, in landscape architecture, a dyke would be constructed. Detailed drawings are needed to convince a client that the design is viable, buildable, and functional. In most cases, a designer creates two to three proposals to be presented to a client.

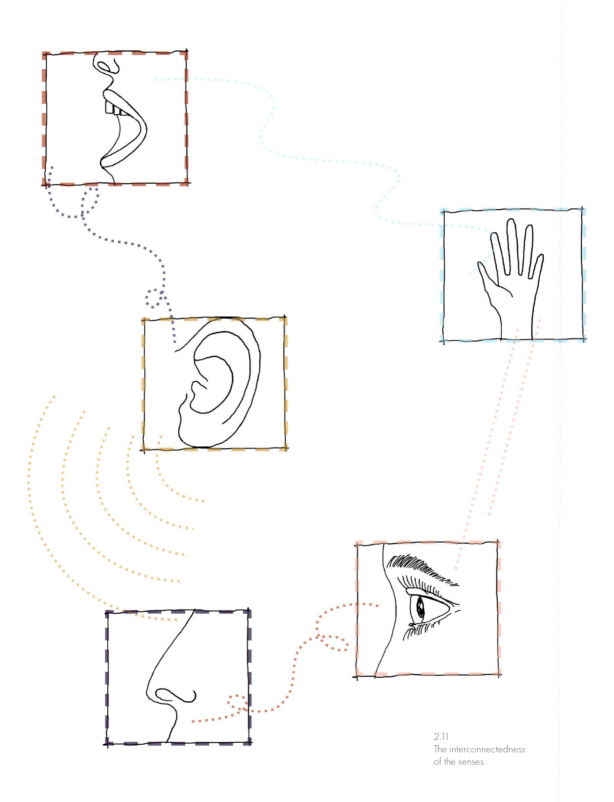

2.11
The interconnectedness of the senses

35

Methods for Interpreting the Senses
A seeing framework for spatial designers

Before beginning a design, every designer must understand the environment in which they will design. Architecture, landscape architecture, planning, industrial design, and civil engineering students and practitioners have to observe the environment to understand the design context. Most often, the sense of sight and visual tools are used to study and document the environment. These tools include maps, data, graphs, diagrams, visual notes (analytical and referential hand or digital representation and field sketches), photography (aerial or eye level views) and videos. However, this method is visually driven and often excludes the other four senses. This is because the other four senses can be difficult to conceptualize, observe, record, and document. Now, with handheld digital recording devices, more ways to record these senses exist at our fingertips. This allows for multisensorial observation to be carried out and recorded more easily than ever before.

Including the other senses is important, as they make the observations and design outcomes more multisensorially inclusive. For example, how can people that are deaf or hard of hearing be notified of a fire while asleep if they are unable to hear the sounds of smoke detectors and fire alarms? Many deaths occur due to deaf or hard of hearing persons not hearing the smoke alarm (Lipps, 2018, p. 119). Japanese researchers developed a fire alarm that emits wasabi, which physically irritates the nose enough to wake humans up in the event of an emergency (Lipps, 2018, p. 119). Without understanding the multisensorial context and having an understanding of the senses and how they work, the industrial designers and researchers could not have come up with this idea. Multisensorial thinking creates innovative and holistic designs.

Thinking multisensorially is important for the following reasons:

- To understand the recording and visualization tools of the individual senses;
- To understand how an individual sense can be cross-referenced with another;
- To understand how an individual sense can be analysed and visualized with the help of other senses, for example using visual representation to describe the intensity and spatiality of smell.

The advantage of multisensorial analysis is that it also introduces a myriad of new analysis tools. Smart phones and tablets offer a readily available method of recording digital sound and movement, providing a layer of valuable information to designers. For instance, "soundscape" mapping could help landscape architects to understand the sounds of an ecosystem. The recordings of certain bird species on a site could help to determine if an ecosystem is healthy or not. An analysis of man-made vs. natural sounds could indicate if a space is imbalanced. Restorative gardens already aspire to this (Mooney, 2020, p. 32), but shouldn't the design of all parks, buildings, and objects aspire to do this as well?

The methods demonstrated in the following pages offer a series of recording and visualization tools to document and design using the senses. This methodology for site observation, recording, and analysis must be gradually taught and practiced throughout the span of an entire design degree. In all design studios this should be regularly applied. With the additional digital tools available, we are now able to observe the environment more precisely. To practice this approach to design, it is crucial to supplement young designers' personal knowledge with multisensorial observation exercises as suggested in Chapter 4.

Recording and Visualizing the Senses

The following table focuses on methods to record and visualize the senses during site observation, perception, and analysis of design. These recording and visualization tools allow students to record their observations and think about how the senses interact spatially. These tools can be applied at all scales, from an object, to a site, to a neighbourhood, to an entire region.

The goals of this table are:

- To develop an understanding of how the senses operate at different scales—from an object, to a site, to a neighbourhood, to a region;
- To develop an understanding of how the senses interact in a spatial context;
- To develop a heightened awareness of space;
- To develop an understanding of what tools to use in the observation and analysis phase of a design;
- To develop an understanding of what tools to use to record and visualize the different senses.

It is important to note that the following table is not exhaustive, and the techniques listed are merely suggestions. Students are encouraged to explore any avenue to which they feel called as they immerse themselves in their environments.

	Recording Tools	Visualization	

Sight
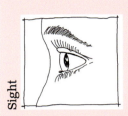

Recording Tools:
- Visual notes
- Photo
- Video
- Mapping
- Aerial map
- Drone imagery
- Text

Visualization:
- Section
- Plan
- Axonometric drawing
- Perspective
- 3D Digital modelling
- Mapping
- Analytical diagrams
- Model making
- Photography
- Video
- Photomontage
- Collage
- Creative writing

Touch
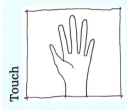

Recording Tools:
- Visual notes
- Photo
- Video
- Mapping
- Material collection
- Text

Visualization:
- Section
- Axonometric
- 3D printing
- Touch mapping
- Collage
- Creative writing
- Descriptive writing
- Model
- Audio recording
- Photo
- Video
- Photomontage

Sound
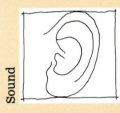

Recording Tools:
- Audio recording
- Visual notes
- Photo
- Video
- Mapping
- Text

Visualization:
- Graph
- Sound mapping
- Plan
- Perspective
- Material maps
- Collage
- Model 1:1
- Audio recording
- Music
- Dance
- Photography
- Video
- Photomontage
- Creative writing

Smell
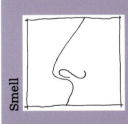

Recording Tools:
- Visual notes
- Photo
- Video
- Mapping
- Material collection
- Text

Visualization:
- Mapping
- Collage
- Creative writing
- Annotated drawings
- Diagram
- Photo
- Video
- Photomontage
- Audio recording
- Creative writing

Taste
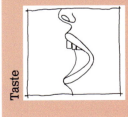

Recording Tools:
- Visual notes
- Photo
- Video
- Mapping
- Audio recording
- Text

Visualization:
- Personal experience
- Diagram
- Section
- Axonometric
- Creative writing
- Collage
- Mapping
- Model
- Audio recording
- Photo
- Video photomontage

38

Analyzing the Interaction of the Senses

This table encourages analytical thinking by cross-referencing between the different senses. This should help to understand the multisensorial spatial experience of the environment's essence. The senses never work individually; they always work consciously or unconsciously in combination with other senses. When practicing environmental observations and perception, one should consciously begin with an individual sense first and then synthesize. The other senses to synthesize are mentioned in each sense category.

The goals of this table are:

- To develop an understanding of how the senses interact with one another;
- To develop a comprehensive understanding of the senses and their impacts on the body and space;
- To adopt the importance of mindfulness as a process in site immersion and analysis;
- To develop a detailed vocabulary to describe different sensorial experiences for objects and sites.

The following tables provide suggestions for how individual sense perception and sensation can be described and represented in combination with other senses. Sight can be represented referentially; while the others can only be represented analytically.

The following table demonstrates how an object might be analyzed by referring to the senses:

	Sight	Touch	Sound	Smell	Taste
Strawberry	shiny, red	bumpy	squishy	sweet	sweet, tart
Banana	yellow	smooth, pasty	n/a	sweet	sweet
Potato chips	round, yellow	flaky, gritty	crunch	fresh	salty
Wooden chair	silver, light form	sandy	clunky	wood, resin	n/a

The same logic can be used during site immersion:

	Sight	Touch	Sound	Smell	Taste
Remedial garden	lush, green	soft, smooth	rustling	herbal, floral	herbal
Vegetable garden	colourful, dense	soft	crunchy, rustling	earth, sweet	earthy, sweet, sour
Medieval church	dark, shadow	cold, damp, wet	echo	musty, moldy	musty
Arid ecosystem	hilly, sandy, earth tones	dry, hot, cold, gritty	muted, wind, hawks	dry, fruity	dry

The diagrams on the following pages further highlight this interaction.

The Sensorial Analysis of a Strawberry

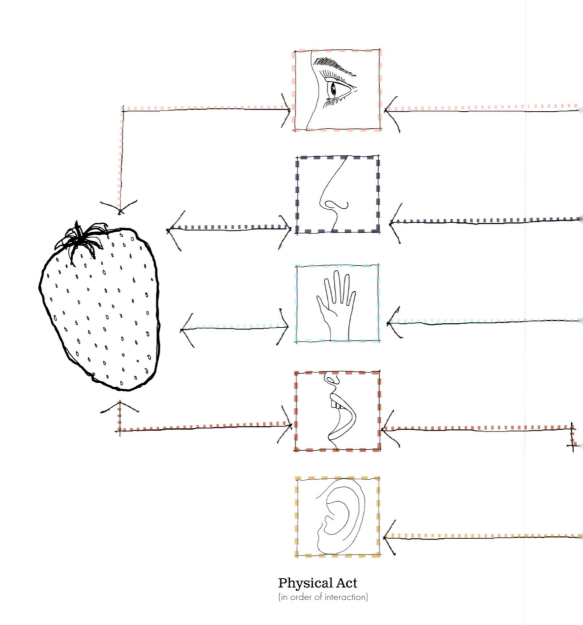

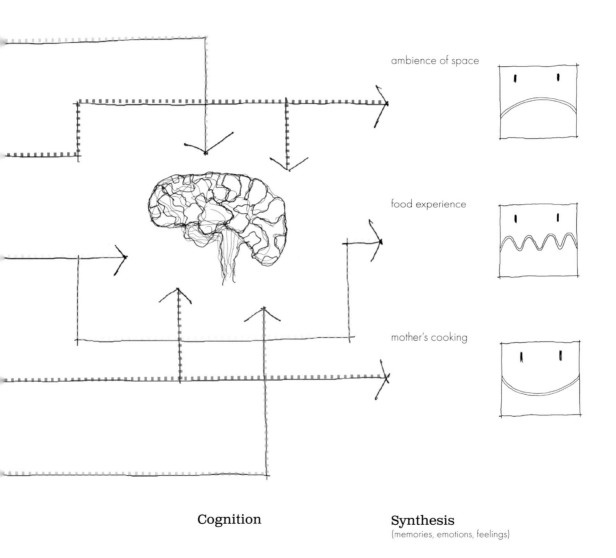

Cognition Synthesis
(memories, emotions, feelings)

Perception

The Sensorial Analysis of a Landscape

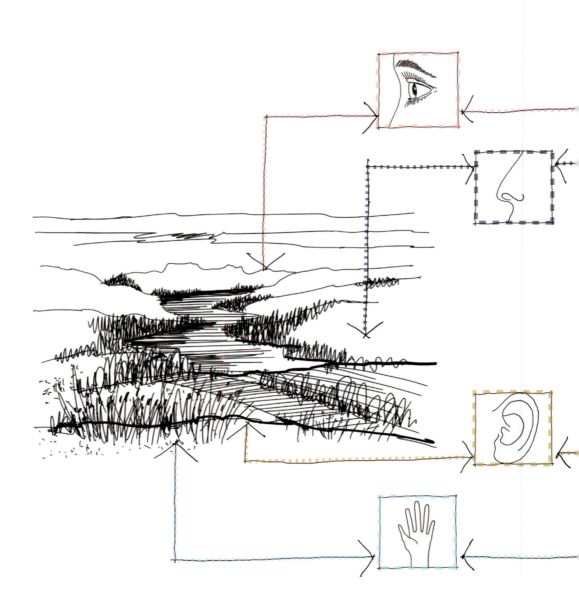

Observation

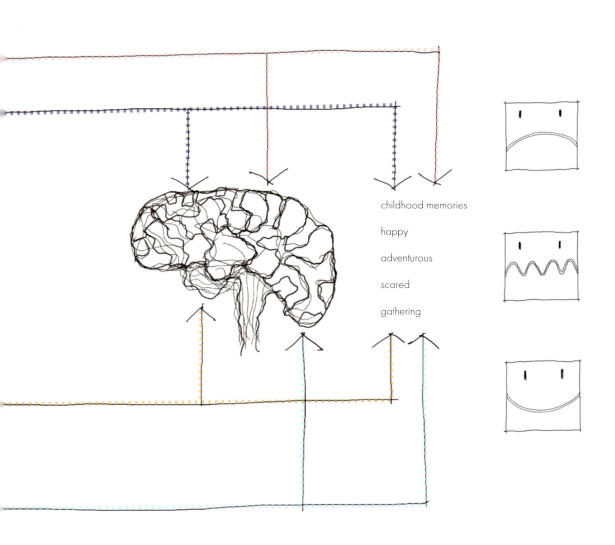

Cognition   Synthesis
            (memories, emotions, feelings)

Perception

44

Sensorial Design Synthesizing List

The *Sensorial Design Synthesizing List* is a suggested checklist to include multisensorial design problem solving and initiate future visions for the design problem. After the design environment and its context have been understood and documented through the *Multisensorial Perception Recording and Visualization Tools*, the next step is to continue with a multi-sensory inclusive design process. The following uses the sensory information acquired through site analysis to do that. The icons suggested can be aligned to the senses one feels and should be prioritized at the beginning of the design, then synthesized with the others. This list acts as a reminder for the designer to include the five main senses in the design ideation process.

1. What is the design problem and its scale?
   - Region
   - Neighbourhood
   - Block
   - Site
   - Object

2. Visualize the design problem diagrammatically
   - Plan
   - Section
   - Perspective
   - Axonometric
   - 3D model
   - Elevation
   - Video
   - Photography
   - Photomontage
   - Etc.

3. Rank the senses given the design problem. During this process, consider users who might not have access to certain senses and how this limitation might shift their design needs.

4. Prioritize importance to design problem and list sensory considerations
    - For example, the design of a fence

Sense Priority	Sensory Considerations
1. Touch	Physical comfort, texture of materiality
2. Sight	Form: light or heavy structure, moving or fixed
3. Smell	Materiality, site surroundings
4. Sound	Sound of wood, plastic, steel, leather, etc.
5. Taste	n/a

5. List further design questions
    - Material
    - Form
    - Surface texture
    - Durability
    - Use
    - Cost
    - Etc.

6. Begin design process

The following pages include several examples for how this list can be used; from a chair to a garden.

A Chair

1. What is the design problem and its scale?
   - Object
   - Design problem: creating a chair for outdoor seating, comfortable, durable, light, easy to handle

2. Visualize the design problem diagrammatically

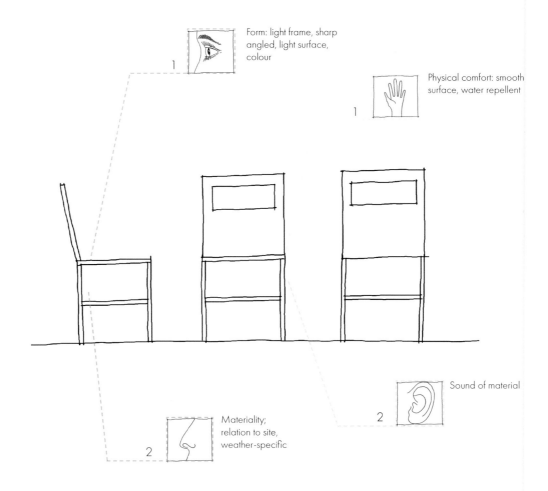

3. Rank the senses given the design problem

   at first glance:

   1 　1 　2 　3

   when considering the visually impaired:

   1 　1 　2 　3

4. Prioritize importance to design problem and list sensory considerations

   sensorial design priority for the visually impaired:

Sense Priority	Sensory Considerations
1. Touch	Physical comfort: smooth surface, water repellent
2. Smell	Materiality: related to site, smell changes due to weather
3. Sound	Sound of material
4. Sight	Form: light frame, sharp angled, light surface, colour

5. List further design questions
   - Material—locally sourced, recyclable?
   - Form—modern, classic, contemporary?
   - Surface texture—smooth painted or not?
   - Durability—materiality: wood, steel, plastic or aluminum?
   - Use outside on soft or stable ground, does it need to be stored and stacked at night?
   - Cost—who is the client public or private?

A Fence

1. What is the design problem and its scale?
   - Object
   - Design problem: creating a fence to safeguard a garden from animals; should show plants on approach; care should be taken to consider those who are visually impaired

2. Visualize the design problem diagrammatically

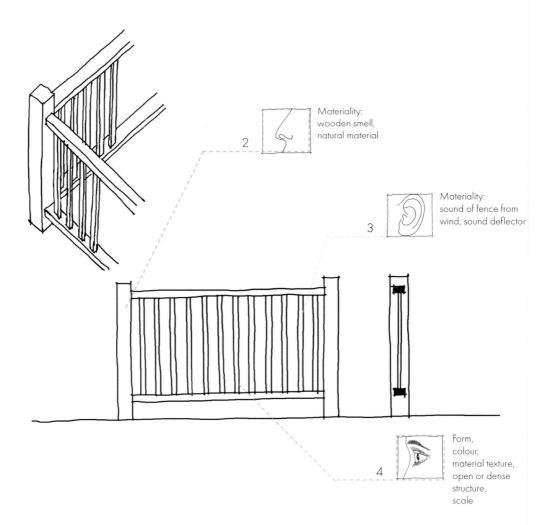

3. Rank the senses given the design problem

   at first glance:

   1 2 3 4

   when considering the visually impaired:

   2 4 3 1

4. Prioritize importance to design problem and list sensory considerations

Sense Priority	Sensory Considerations
1. Touch	Materiality: soft surface, wood surface, rounded edges, etc.
2. Sound	Materiality: sound of fence from wind, sound deflector
3. Smell	Materiality: wooden smell, natural material
4. Sight	Form, colour, material texture, open or dense structure, scale

5. List further design questions
   - Material—locally sourced, recyclable?
   - Form—relating to surrounding context?
   - Surface texture—smooth or rough, painted or not?
   - Durability—materiality: wood, steel, plastic or aluminum?
   - Use—public or private use, vandalism, safety, reduce sharp edges
   - Cost—who is the client, public or private?

A Partitioning Wall

1. What is the design problem and its scale?
   - Site / building
   - Design problem: designing a partition wall in a building that is light weight, sustainable, with no use of chemicals, care should be taken to consider those who have allergies

2. Visualize the design problem diagrammatically

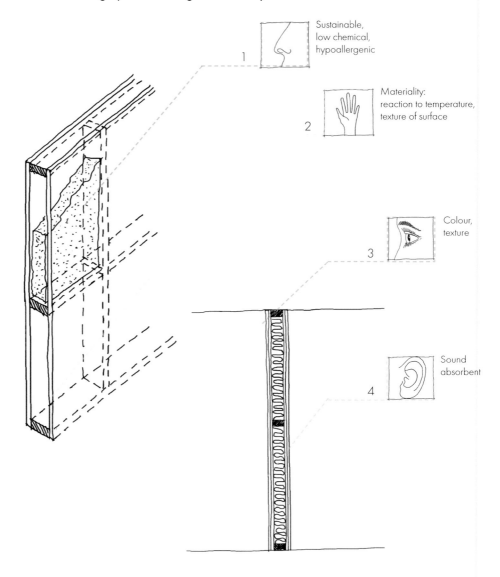

3. Rank the senses given the design problem

   at first glance:

   1 2 3 4

   when considering those with allergies:

   3 2 1 4

4. Prioritize importance to design problem and list sensory considerations

Sense Priority for those sensitive to allergens	Sensory Considerations
1. Smell	Sustainable, low chemical, hypoallergenic
2. Touch	Materiality: reaction to temperature, texture of surface
3. Sight	Colour, texture
4. Sound	Sound absorbant

5. List further design questions
   - Cost
   - Material—locally sourced, recyclable?
   - Surface texture—smooth or rough, painted?
   - Durability—material wood, aluminum and plasterboard?
   - Use—inside public or private use, room sound activity—domestic, commercial?

A Garden

1. What is the design problem and its scale?
   - Site
   - Design problem: designing a pocket garden easily accessible for the a visually impaired person

2. Visualize the design problem diagrammatically

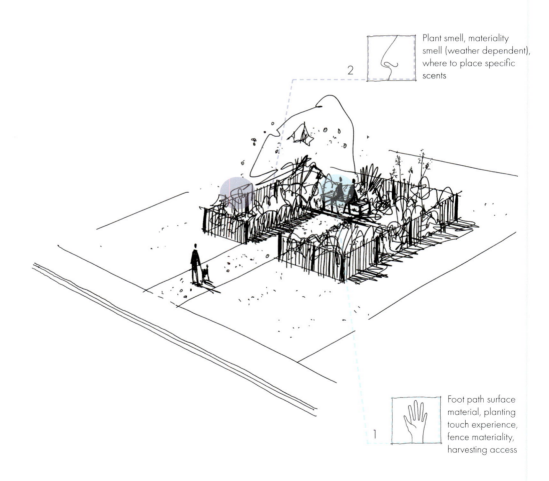

Plant smell, materiality smell (weather dependent), where to place specific scents

Foot path surface material, planting touch experience, fence materiality, harvesting access

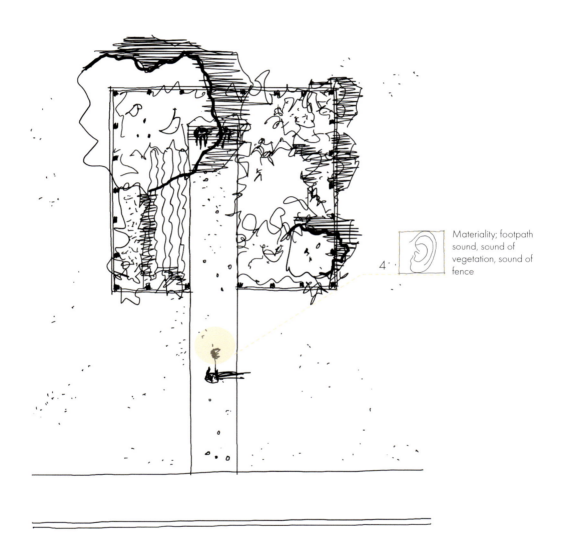

Materiality; footpath sound, sound of vegetation, sound of fence

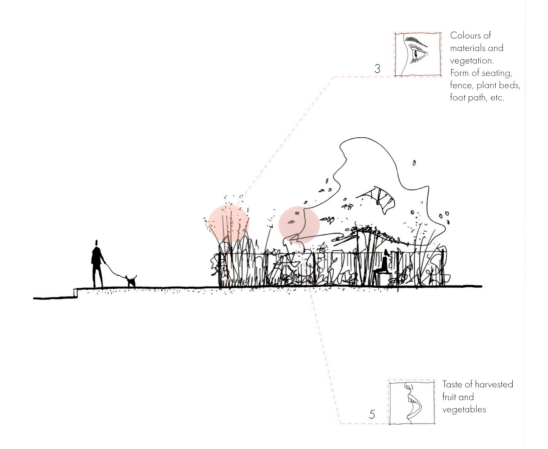

Colours of materials and vegetation. Form of seating, fence, plant beds, foot path, etc.

Taste of harvested fruit and vegetables

3. Rank the senses given the design problem

Sensory hierarchy in garden entrance/approach, when considering those who are visually impaired:

Sensory hierarchy inside the garden:

4. Prioritize importance to design problem and list sensory considerations

Sense Priority	Sensory Considerations
1. Smell	Plant smell Materiality smell (weather dependent) Where to place specific scents
2. Touch	Foot path surface material Planting touch experience Fence materiality Harvesting access
3. Sight	Colours of materials and vegetation Form of seating, fence, plant beds, foot path, etc.
4. Sound	Materiality: footpath sound sound of vegetation sound of fence
5. Taste	Taste of harvested fruit and vegetables

5. List further design questions
    - Materiality of path—soft or hard, small or large, gravel or asphalt?
    - Form of planting—variety of textures, different plant sizes, leaf textures, soft and hard leaves, hairy or glossy leaves?
    - Durability—material wood, steel, plastic or aluminum?
    - Colour—visual experience of plants, fence, path, bench and seasons?
    - Cost—who is the client public or private?

Recommended Reads

The Senses: Design beyond Vision, Ellen Lupton & Andrea Lipps (2018)
This book is a current summary focusing on the main senses beyond vision. It is a concise description of current extraordinary thinkers on multisensorial all-inclusive design practice. This book opens one's eyes, ears, mouth, nose and skin to sense the world holistically. The book provides inspiring ideas and principles for the sensory richness of objects, environment, and media.

Envisioning Information, Edward Tufte (1990)
This book displays beautiful and compelling visuals of highly complex data. The most design oriented of Tufte's books, it presents maps, charts, scientific presentations, diagrams, computer interfaces, statistical graphics and tables, stereo photographs, guidebooks, timetables, uses of colour, and other displays of information. The book provides practical advice about how to explain complex material through visual means, with well-chosen examples to illustrate the fundamental principles of information displays.

Beautiful Evidence, Edward Tufte (2006)
This book provides examples of the ways in which we can display data that are visually coherent and compelling. The book identifies methods for showing multiple types of information, suggests many new designs, and provides analytical tools for assessing the credibility of evidence presentations (which are seen from both sides, such as how to produce and how to consume presentations).

References

Bradford, A. (2017). "The five and more senses". Retrieved from https://www.livescience.com/60752-human-senses.html

Have, R. & van der Toorn, M. (2012). The role of hand drawing in basic design education in the digital age. *International Conference on Engineering and Mathematics*, Bangalore, 2012. Les Ulis, FR: EDP Sciences.

Lipps, A. (2018). Scentscape. In E. Lupton and A. Lipps (Eds.) *The Senses: Design beyond Vision* (pp. 109-121). New York, NY: Princeton Architecture Press.

Lupton, E. (2018). Flavour. In E. Lupton and A. Lipps (Eds.) *The Senses: Design beyond Vision*, ed. Lupton and Lipps (pp. 66-71). New York, NY: Princeton Architecture Press.

Mau, B. (2018). Designing Live. In E. Lupton and A. Lipps (Eds.) *The Senses: Design beyond Vision* (pp. 22). New York, NY: Princeton Architecture Press.

Mooney, P. (2020). *Planting Design: Connecting People and Place*. Abingdon: Routledge.

Pallasmaa, J. (2005). *The Eyes of the Skin*, Chichester: Wiley Publishing.

Patterson, D. & Aftel, M. (2017). *The Art of Flavor: Practices and Principles for Creating Delicious Food*. New York, NY: Riverhead Books.

Chapter 3

Sensewalks

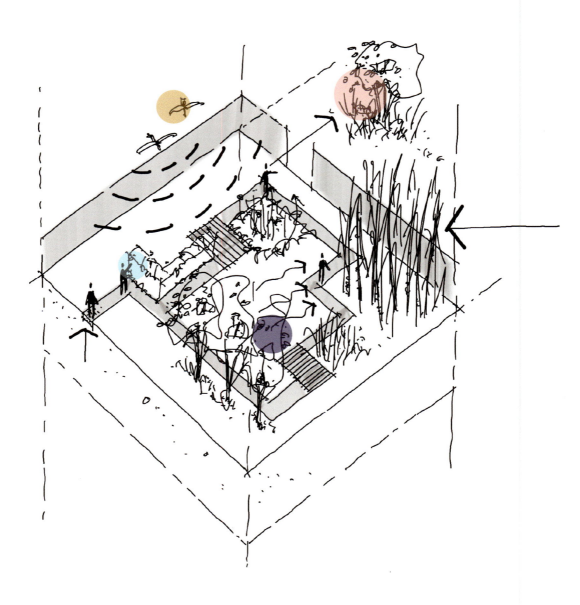

On Sensewalks

This chapter takes a look at real-life applications of multi-sensory design. Through 12 gardens, we will demonstrate how each of these sites engages with the senses. This chapter's mapping was inspired from a book chapter published by the author in 2020 titled "Sense...ible Parks and Gardens" in which he describes the idea of sensewalks, and how these could be a strategy for sensitizing the public to protect ecological and cultural heritage in their neighbourhoods (Roehr, 2020, pp. 81-389).

Sensewalks are not new; they have been experimented with since the early 1960's for research and educational purposes (Henshaw, 2014, p.42). For instance, soundwalks, were first introduced in the early 1970's by Raymond Murray Schafer at Simon Fraser University in Vancouver, Canada (Henshaw, 2014, p. 42). Soundwalking was an attempt to heighten the sensual experience in the environment by intentionally disabling a sense such as sight (through blindfolding) in order to experience sound more deeply. Westerkamp's soundwalking activity guides participants to engage with a space through the description of sound (Westerkamp, 2007, pp. 49-58). Learning to listen was key in familiarizing the participants to a myriad of sounds.

Similar to soundwalks, a researcher at Sheffield University named Victoria Henshaw organizes smellwalks with the general public to research and understand the perception of urban smells. Kate McLean, an artist and scholar also organizes smellwalks and visualizes her participatory findings in smellmaps. Both scholars inspire the public to engage in conscious smelling of the environment. Henshaw organizes smellwalks to consciously switch from a passive perception of smell into a receptive state of "smelling in search," and she uses these findings to formulate strategies to design for urban smell (2014, p. 43). McLean's maps are gathered through shared group interpretation, with an aim of facilitating more exploration and depiction of smells by the public (2018, p. 75). Recent public participatory research and artistic visualization of smell has heightened people's awareness of multisensorial design, demonstrating that the smells of a space are as important as the sounds it makes or its visual appearance. Many historic parks and gardens are an essential part of the urban fabric and are havens for multisensorial exploration of the senses. Combined with their cultural importance, they work like an interactive exhibition or museum of sensory impressions.

The precedents provided give an insight to experiencing sites multisensorially. The precedents presented are provided with a brief historic description with annotated drawings that highlight the multisensorial experiences found in each of these gardens. Our decision to focus on historic and contemporary gardens provides a condensed cultural and historic experience where they are located and often includes buildings such as pavilions, gazebos, and covered pergolas.

Humble Administrator's Garden
Wang Xiancheng
Suzhou, China

The Humble Administrator's Garden is 5.6 hectares, making it the largest ancient Chinese garden in Suzhou. The garden was built during the Ming Dynasty, and is over 500 years old. It was listed as a UNESCO World Heritage Site in 1997.

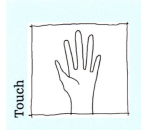

Touch	Flying Rainbow Bridge	Smooth, seamless walking experience; Railings smooth to the touch
	Millet Fragrance Hall	Smooth, seamless walking experience
	The Wave Corridor	Undulating corridor; feel the change in the slope of the ground, smooth surface
	Artificial rockery	A variety of texture experiences, from smooth to gritty

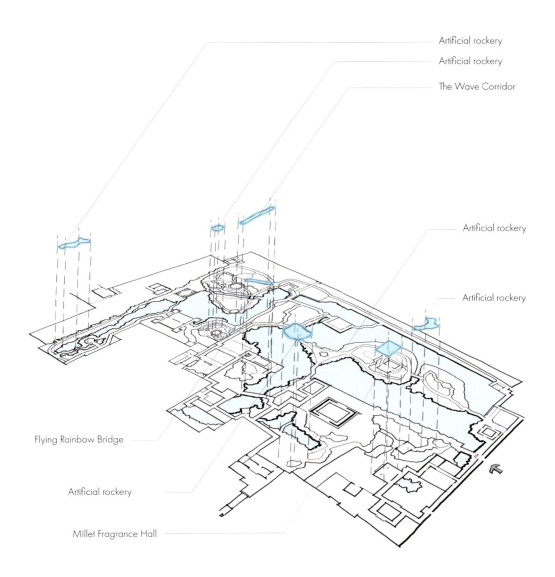

Sound		
	The Pine Wind Pavilion	Light rustling of the pine leaves as wind passes through
	The Rain Veranda	Surrounded by lotus, plantain, and bamboo, you are able to listen to all the different ways in which rain falls on the leaves. From small drops, to gentle thuds, to a shower, you experience an orchestra of sounds.
	The Stay-and-Listen Parlour	Gentle thud of raindrops on lotus leaves
	Snow-Fragrance-and-Rosy-Cloud Pavilion	Peaceful and quiet, peppered with the chirping of birds and the humming of cicadas
	The Malus Spring Castle	Echoes, vast: this space is also where guqin performances take place, as the courtyard amplifies the sound of the stringed instrument.

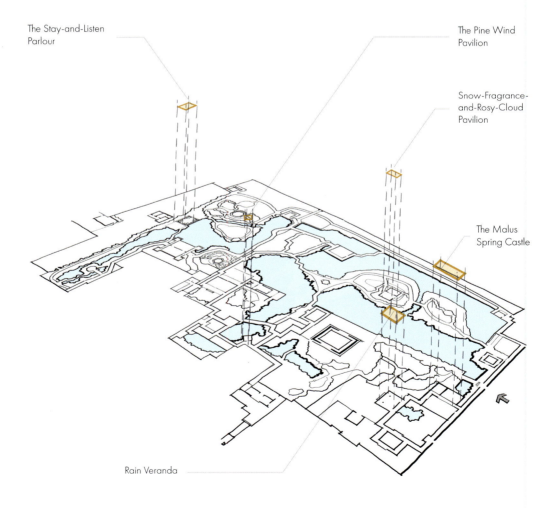

Smell		
	Lotus Chamber	Fresh, fragrant smell of lotuses
	Magnolia Hall	Sweet fragrance of magnolia flowers during the spring
	Xue Xiang Yun Wei Pavilion	Sweet smell of plum blossoms in winter and spring
	Snow-Fragrance-and-Rosy-Cloud Pavilion	Peaceful and quiet, peppered with the chirping of birds and the humming of cicadas
	The Boat-Structure	Fresh, fragrant smell of lotuses
	The Malus Spring Castle	Sweet smell of crab apples as they bloom in the spring
	The Hall of Distant Fragrance	Delicate smell of lotus leaves and flowers

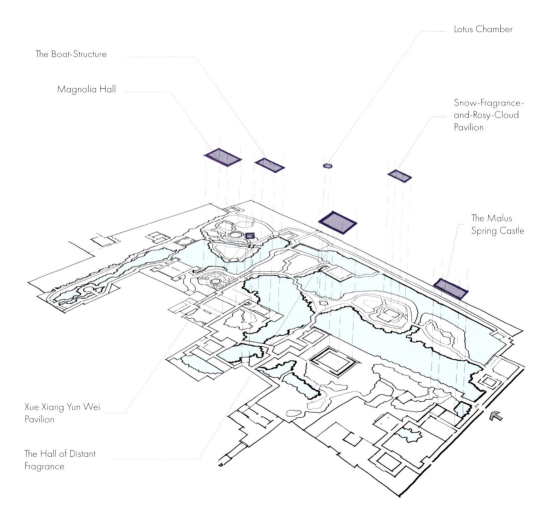

Fin Garden
Kashan, Iran

Fin Garden is a 2.3 hectare historical Persian garden. It was built under the rule of Abbas I of Persia during the 16th century and is known for its wide variety of water features. It is the oldest existing garden in Iran and is a UNESCO World Heritage Site.

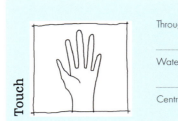

Touch	Throughout the site	Natural stone paving: cold to the touch, bumpy and rough surface on the feet
	Waterways	Cooling, soothing, gentle moving through your fingers
	Central pool	Calm, cold on your hand

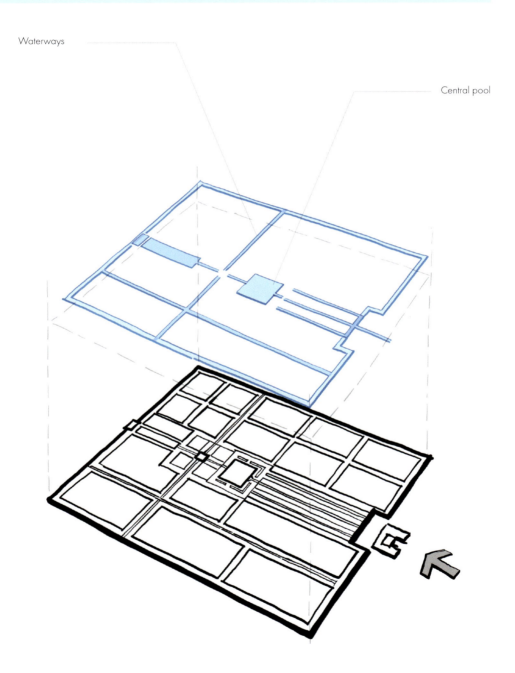

Waterways

Central pool

Sound		
	Throughout the site	All encompassing sound of water
	Long pool	Subtle calm splashing sound of the fountains falling into the water
	Central pool	Calm, peaceful
	Irrigation channels	The gentle trickling of water as it enters the channels
	Water steps	Soft flushing sound
	Safavid Pavilion	Calm, peaceful

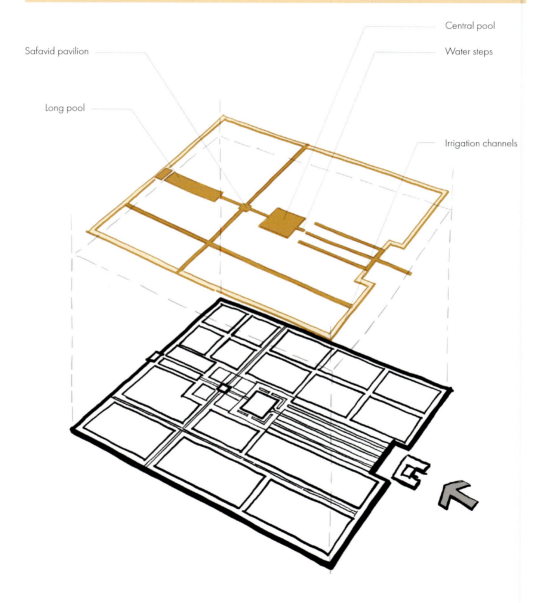

Smell		
	Soil from the garden beds	Earthy, musty
	Throughout the site	Pine and cypress trees: resinous, earthy, fresh, subtly sweet

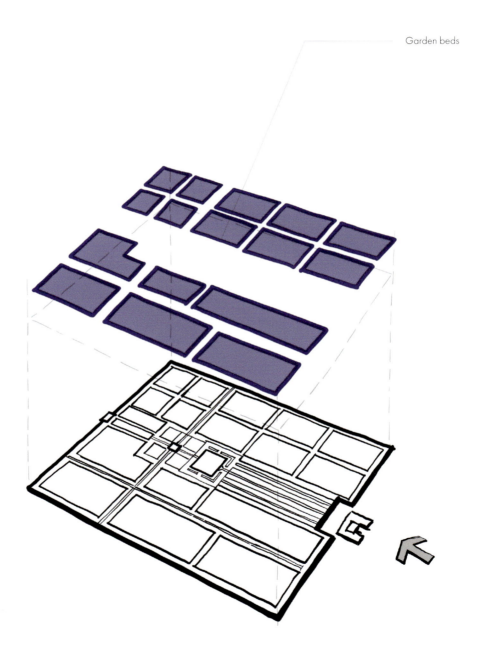

Garden beds

Katsura Imperial Villa Gardens
Prince Hachijō Toshihito
Kyoto, Japan

Built in 1620, the Katsura Imperial Villa Gardens surround the villa of Prince Hachijō Toshihito. Designed by the prince, the 6.9 hectare garden was inspired immensely by passages from The Tales of Genji, a favourite of the prince. It is often revered as the master example of traditional Japanese gardens.

Touch	Tsuzumi waterfall	Refreshing, cool
	Shirakawa-bashi	Stone washing bowls, before entering the tea pavilion, people are required to wash their hands to cleanse the body and mind; cleansing, refreshing, gritty texture, peaceful
	Suhama	Shores of the lake: rough, smooth, gritty, bumpy

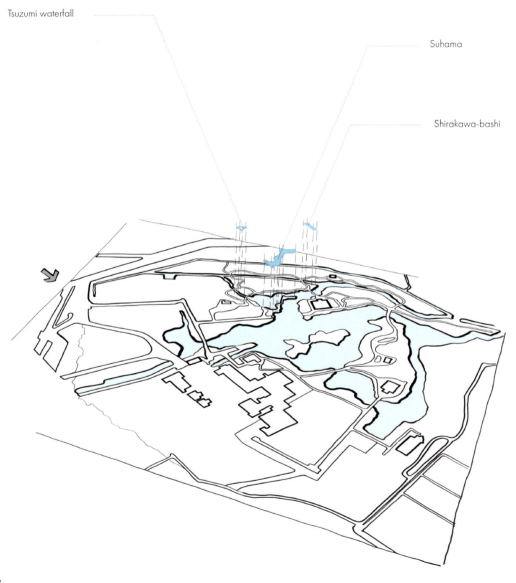

Sound		
	Throughout the site	Rustling of pine needles as the wind moves through them
	Tsuzumi waterfall	Rushing of water, loud, exciting, all-encompassing in its sound
	Shokin-tei	Gentle thud of raindrops on the roof
	Musical instrument room	Echoes when empty, when music is played it fills the room

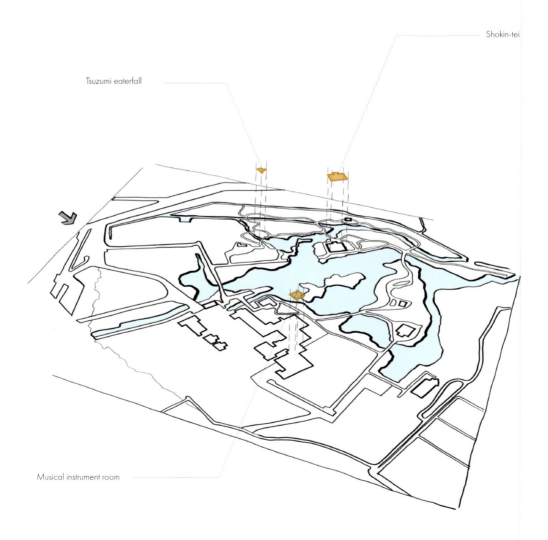

Smell	Throughout the buildings	A dry, sweet, straw-like smell wafts throughout the buildings and the side from the tatami mats
	Tea rooms (Pine-Lute Pavilion, Onrindo, Shoiken)	Muted smell, done purposefully so that the tea fragrance can be thor-oughly experienced while tasting. Tea smell is herbal and sweet
Taste	Tea rooms (Pine-Lute Pavilion, Onrindo, Shoiken)	Herbal, grassy, bitter, toasted, smooth

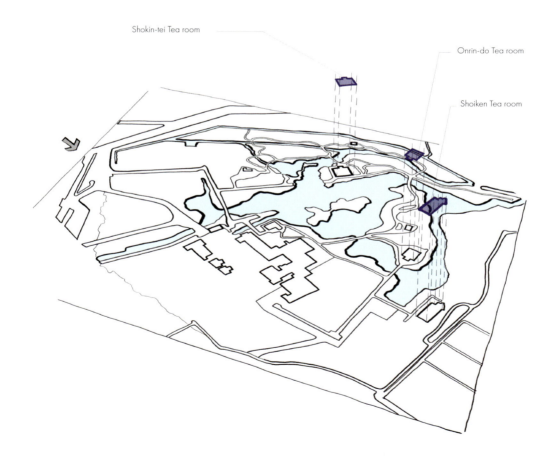

The Monumental Garden of Valsanzibio
Luigi Bernini
Valsanzibio, Italy

Zuane Francesco Barbarigo made a holy vow to create a "masterpiece" as thanks to god for surviving the bubonic plague that prevailed in Italy at the time. Built in the 17th century, these gardens became a place of refuge and redemption, complete with vistas, fountains, and statues. The 16 hectare gardens are considered to be one of the most culturally significant gardens in Italy.

Touch

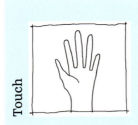

Labyrinth	Boxwood feels textured, smooth, soft
Marble table	Smooth, cold
The fountains of the gardens	Moist, cool to the skin
Gravel pathways	Gritty

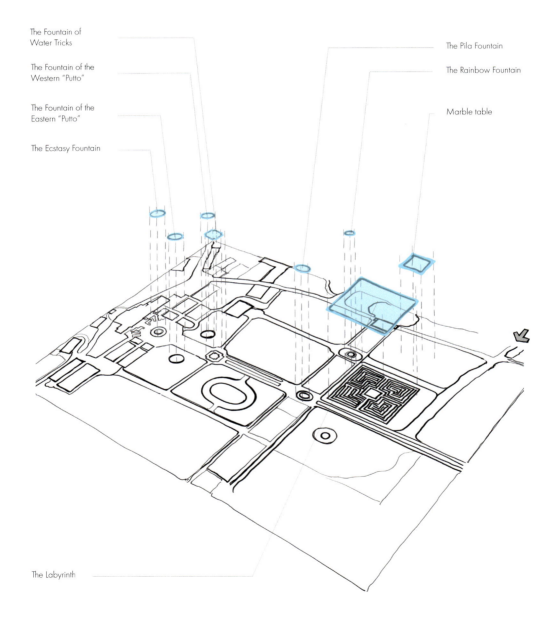

The Fountain of Water Tricks

The Fountain of the Western "Putto"

The Fountain of the Eastern "Putto"

The Ecstasy Fountain

The Pila Fountain

The Rainbow Fountain

Marble table

The Labyrinth

76

Sound		
	The fountains of the gardens	Splashing, trickling of water
	Throughout the site	The crunching from the gravel pathways; rustling of boxwood and hornbeam leaves in the wind

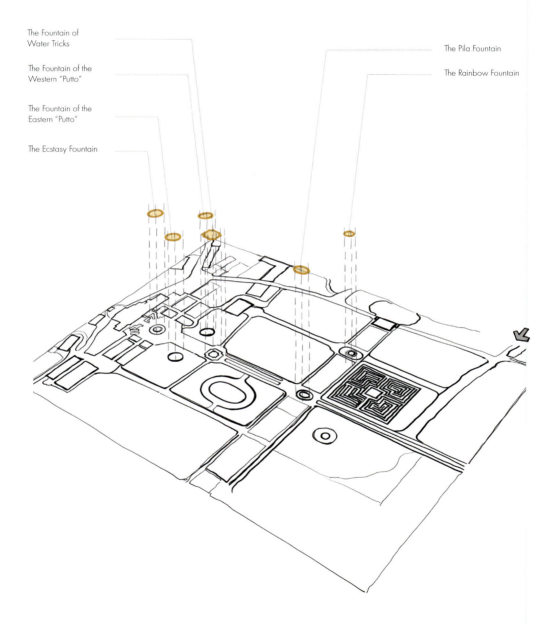

The Fountain of Water Tricks

The Fountain of the Western "Putto"

The Fountain of the Eastern "Putto"

The Ecstasy Fountain

The Pila Fountain

The Rainbow Fountain

Smell

Ponds	Musky
The fountains of the gardens	Clean, fresh
Labyrinth	Resinous, musky, pine-line

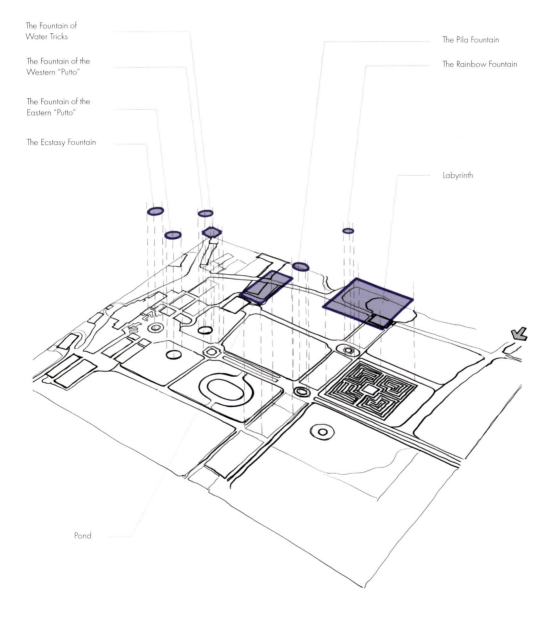

- The Fountain of Water Tricks
- The Fountain of the Western "Putto"
- The Fountain of the Eastern "Putto"
- The Ecstasy Fountain
- The Pila Fountain
- The Rainbow Fountain
- Labyrinth
- Pond

Hidcote Manor Garden

Lawrence Johnston
Chipping Campden, United Kingdom

Lawrence Johnston was an esteemed garden designer in the United Kingdom who purchased Hidcote Manor for him and his mother to live in. Strongly influenced by the Arts and Crafts movement, Johnston designed the garden in 1905 to include several garden rooms around the house, with each serving its own purpose. He was also a horticulturalist and made an effort to showcase plants from all over the world at Hidcote. Hidcote was transferred to the National Trust in 1947.

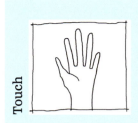

Touch		
	The bathing pool garden	Cool atmosphere surrounding the fountain
	The red borders and gazebos	Stone steps, gravel, and lawn make up the trails, so that the trail experience shifts from smooth, to gritty, to soft
	The plant house	Warm, humid atmosphere

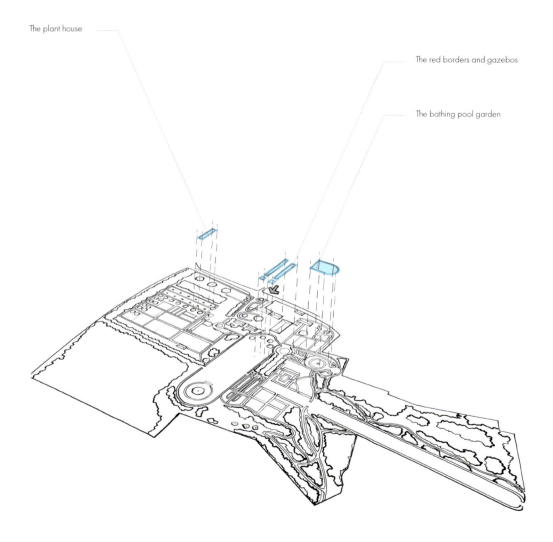

The plant house

The red borders and gazebos

The bathing pool garden

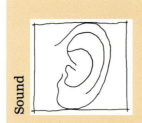

Sound

The old garden	Chirping of birds, buzzing of insects
The bathing pool garden	Trickling of water

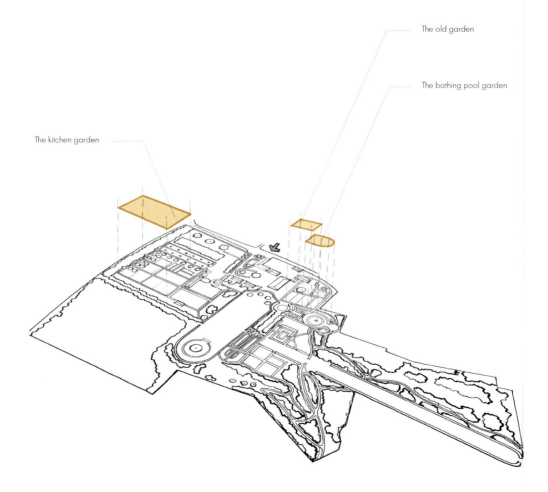

The old garden

The bathing pool garden

The kitchen garden

Smell			
		The rose walk	Smell of roses, floral, sweet, all encompassing
		The white garden	Floral, fragrant, soft
		The plant house	Earthy, fresh, fragrant in spring
		The old garden	Floral, fragrant, sweet
		The kitchen garden	Herbal, earthy

Taste			
		The kitchen garden	Earthy, herbal, sweet, fresh

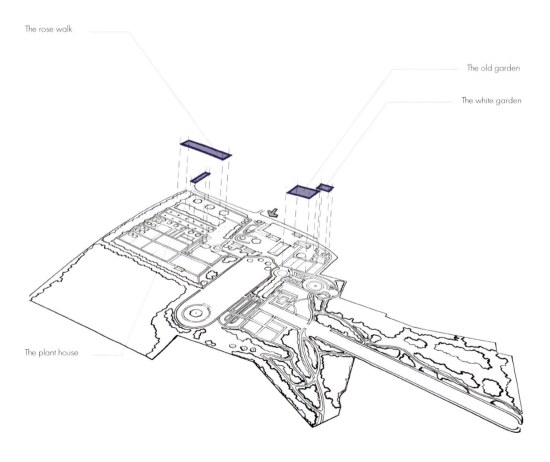

Villandry Gardens
Alix de Saint-Venant
Villandry, France

The garden surrounds the château of Villandry. It is an example of a formal French garden of the Renaissance, with its symmetrical layout and box hedging. The garden is divided into four parts: the sun garden, the kitchen garden, the water garden, and the ornamental garden. The gardens were destroyed in the 19th century and restored in 1908 by Joachim Carvallo.

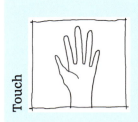

Touch		
	Gravel pathways	Gritty
	The Audience Pavilion	Warmth, comfort
	The maze	Boxed hedges feel textured, smooth, soft
	The Water Garden	Cool atmosphere

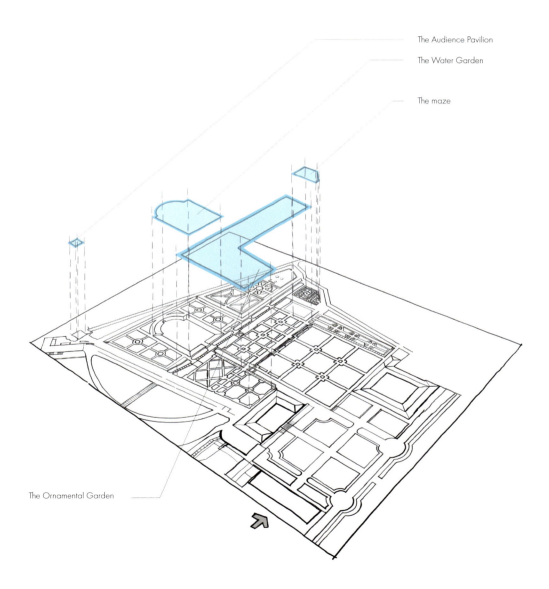

The Audience Pavilion
The Water Garden
The maze
The Ornamental Garden

Sound		
	The woodland	Gentle rustling of the leaves as the wind blows through them
	The Water Garden	Trickling water over steps, calm and quiet around the pond, splashing of the fountains
	The Ornamental Garden	Chirping of birds, buzzing of insects, rustling of leaves in the wind

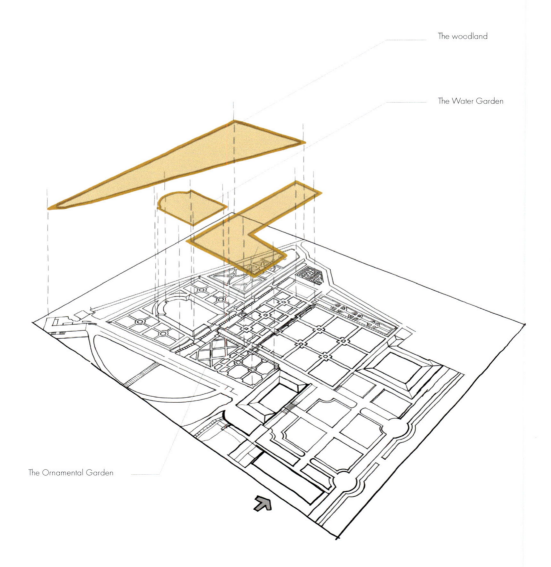

The woodland

The Water Garden

The Ornamental Garden

Smell		
	The Kitchen Garden	Earthy, herbal, floral, sweet
	The Sun Garden	Floral, fragrant
	The Herb Garden	Herbal, earthy, floral, fresh

Taste		
	The Kitchen Garden	Earthy, herbal, sweet, fresh

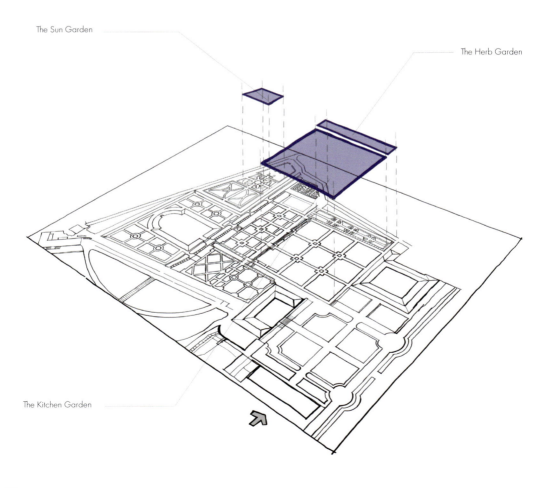

William E. Carter School Sensory Garden

David Berarducci
Boston, United States

This garden design was developed for a school that teaches students with physical and learning disabilities. The school needed a space for youth to be able to learn and ground themselves outdoors. The garden was designed in 2002 with spaces for learning to grow plants, group activities, and visual mobility training.

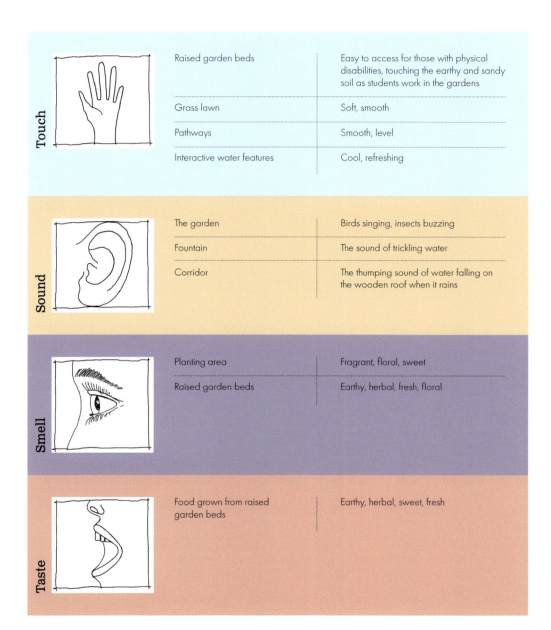

Touch		Raised garden beds	Easy to access for those with physical disabilities, touching the earthy and sandy soil as students work in the gardens
		Grass lawn	Soft, smooth
		Pathways	Smooth, level
		Interactive water features	Cool, refreshing
Sound		The garden	Birds singing, insects buzzing
		Fountain	The sound of trickling water
		Corridor	The thumping sound of water falling on the wooden roof when it rains
Smell		Planting area	Fragrant, floral, sweet
		Raised garden beds	Earthy, herbal, fresh, floral
Taste		Food grown from raised garden beds	Earthy, herbal, sweet, fresh

Oizumi Ryokuchi Park

Yoshisuke Miyake
Osaka, Japan

In the 1970s the "Garden of the Blind" was designed specifically for people who were visually impaired. It was redesigned in the 1990s to become a garden that engaged all the senses. Designers engaged with roughly 500 people to determine which features would be most inclusive for the park. Within the sensory garden there is the "Garden of the Kitchen," the "Garden of Sound," the "Garden of Colour," and the "Garden of Scent."

Touch	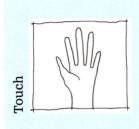	Raised planting beds	Easy access to touch and engage with a myriad of plants and water features
		Displays	Tactile, easy to understand and learn from them
		Daquan Pond	Coolness from the water
		Raised pool	Cool
		Sculptures	Smooth, cold
Sound	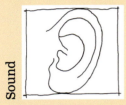	Throughout the garden	Birds chirping, insects buzzing
		Garden of Sound	Musical; clay pots buried in the soil make different sounds when water drips on them
Smell	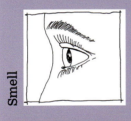	Grassland	Fresh, herbal
		Plant beds	Fragrant, floral, sweet
		Garden of smell	Fragrant, floral, sweet, earthy
Taste		Garden of the Kitchen	Earthy, herbal, sweet, fresh

The Garden of Five Senses

Pradeep Sachdeva Architects
Delhi, India

A landmark in Delhi, The Garden of Five Senses was designed to create engagement between humans and nature. Built in 2003, the park encompasses a wide range of activities, from contemplation and relaxation, to cultural events and shopping.

Touch	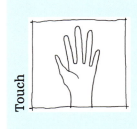	Sculptures of different materials	Touch the sculpture to experience the texture of different materials
		Pathways	Gritty, smooth, level, bumpy
		Khas Bagh (the spiral walkway)	Winding, steady, smooth
		Water features	Cool atmosphere
Sound	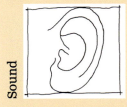	Grassland	Herbal, fresh
		Gardens	Fragrant, floral, herbal, sweet, fresh
		In-park restaurants	Aromatic, all encompassing
Smell	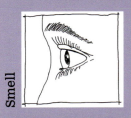	Bell trees	Singing of bells as the wind blows through the trees
		Bamboo courtyard	Quiet, still, wind
		Water features	Trickling, splashing of the fountains
Taste	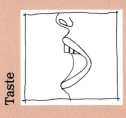	In-park restaurants	Salty, sweet, spicy, bitter, sour

Eins + Alles-Experience Field of the Senses
Welzheim, Germany

Wholly inspired by Hugo Kükelhaus's Experience Field of the Senses pavilion that he designed for Expo 67, this park engages with both restoration and play through the senses. Located in a natural reserve, there are 80 sensory stations designed for individuals to engage with natural elements and the senses.

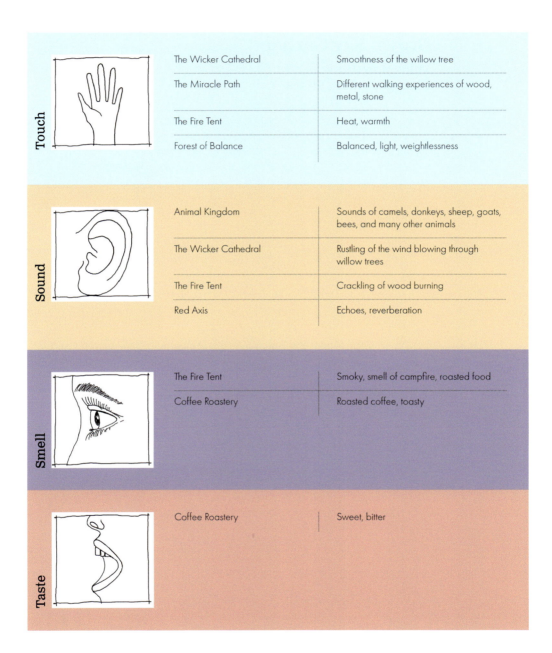

Crown Sky Garden

Mikyoung Kim
Chicago, United States

Located on the 23rd storey of Chicago's Children's Hospital, the Crown Sky Garden was built to be a space for healing. A great deal of research was conducted prior to its design, establishing links between access to nature and healthy recovery. The indoor design examines how green space may be accessible and restorative for all.

Touch

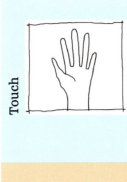

Resin Wall	Smooth
Reclaimed wood seating	Smooth
Bubbler Fountain	Bubbly, bumpy, cool
Bamboo Grove	Smooth, soft
River Rock	Rough, gritty

Sound

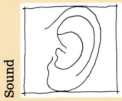

Resin Wall	Interactive sound
Bubbler Fountain	Bubbling sound of water
Center of garden	Musical performances, echoes

Smell

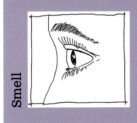

Reclaimed wood sculptures	Pine, resinous
Bamboo Grove	Fresh, herbal

The Elizabeth and Nona Evans Restorative Garden

Dirtworks Landscape Architects
Cleveland, United States

A component of the Cleveland Botanical Garden, the Elizabeth and Nona Evans Restorative Garden was created to be a space of accessibility, education, restoration, and comfort. Built in 1998, the garden is divided into three parts: the Contemplative Garden, the Horticultural Therapy Garden, and the Garden for Learning and Exploring.

Touch	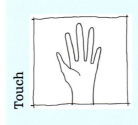	Pathway	Comfortable width and paving to allow for all types of mobility to move smoothly throughout each space
		Horticultural therapy garden	Planting beds were made at levels that could be touched and engaged with by people who use wheelchairs
		Stone walls	Gritty, rough, smooth
		Railings	Braille inserts have been added to the outer edge of the railing with a poem
		Grass lawn	Soft, comfortable
Sound	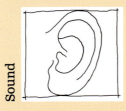	Throughout the gardens	Birds chirping and insects buzzing
		Garden for learning and exploring	Trickling water, exciting, lively
		Contemplative garden	Peaceful, quiet
Smell	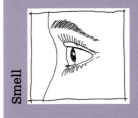	Horticultural therapy garden	Floral, herbal, fresh; the basil walk is all consuming in its herbal smell, with a variety of basil plants lining the pathway.
		Grass lawn	Grassy, herbal, earthy
		Rose Garden	Fragrant, floral, sweet

References

AHTAVideos. (2008, November 9). *The William E. Carter School Sensory Garden Classroom* [video]. YouTube. Retrieved from https://www.youtube.com/watch?v=2ouC2a4LhQM

American Society of Landscape Architects. (2006). *General Design Award of Honor: The Elizabeth & Nona Evans restorative garden*. Retrieved from https://www.asla.org/awards/2006/06winners/294.html

American Society of Landscape Architects. (2013). *The Crown Sky Garden: Ann and Robert H. Lurie Children's Hospital of Chicago*. Retrieved from https://www.asla.org/2013awards/374.html

Château Villandry. (n.d.). *The History of Villandry*. Retrieved from https://www.chateauvillandry.fr/en/explore/the-history-of-villandry/

David Berarducci Landscape Architecture. (n.d.). *W. E. Carter School Sensory Garden*. Retrieved from http://www.db-la.com/w.e.%20carter%20school.htm

Dirtworks Landscape Architecture. (n.d.). *Elizabeth and Nona Evans Restorative Garden*. Retrieved from https://dirtworks.us/portfolio/99-elizabeth-nona-evans-restorative-garden-2/

Eins + Alles. (n.d.). *Places*. Retrieved from https://www.eins-und-alles.de/orte

Faghih, N., & Sadeghy, A. (2012). Persian gardens and landscapes. *Architectural Design, 82*(3), 38-51. doi: 10.1002/ad.1403

Falcondale, J. (2017). *A Hard Lesson in Garden Design from Château Villandry*. Retrieved from https://falcondalelife.com/garden-design-chateau-villandry/

George B. Henderson Foundation. (n.d.). *Special Projects: Sensory Garden*. Retrieved from http://thehendersonfoundation.com/sensory_garden.htm

Guidento. (2016, August 9). *Garden Five Sense Delhi Tourist Attractions* [video]. YouTube. Retrieved from https://www.youtube.com/watch?v=KF5YDy3oKtA

Henshaw, V (2014). *Urban Smellscapes: Understanding and Designing City Smell Environments*. New York, NY: Routledge.

Holmes, D. (2013). Crown Sky Garden, Mikyoung Kim Design. *World Landscape Architect*. Retrieved from https://worldlandscapearchitect.com/crown-sky-garden-chicago-usa-mikyoung-kim-design/

Jackson, M. (2020). *Hidcote: An Arts and Crafts-Inspired Garden*. Retrieved from https://mikejackson1948.blog/2020/04/01/hidcote-an-arts-and-craft-inspired-garden/

Kamp, D. (2009). *Creating Restorative Settings: Inclusive Design Considerations*. Retrieved from https://www.nrs.fs.fed.us/pubs/gtr/gtr-nrs-p-39papers/08-kamp-p-39.pdf

Luescher, A. (2006). Experience field for the development of the senses: Hugo Kükelhaus' phenomenology of consciousness. *The International Journal of Art & Design Education, 25*(1), 67-73. https://doi.org/10.1111/j.1476-8070.2006.00469.x

Lurie Children's Hospital of Chicago. (n.d.). *Crown Sky Garden*. Retrieved from https://www.luriechildrens.org/en/patients-visitors/explore-the-hospital/crown-sky-garden/

McLean, K. (2018). "Communicating and mediating smellscapes: The design and exposition of olfactory mappings." In V. Henshaw, K. McLean, D. Medway, C. Perkins, & G. Warnaby

(Eds.) *Designing with Smell: Practices, Techniques and Challenges* (pp. 67-77). New York, NY: Routledge.

Med-o-Med. (2012). *Inventory of Islamic Historic Gardens: Fin Garden in Iran*. Retrieved from https://medomed.org/2012/fin-garden-in-iran-2/

Mikyoung Kim Design. (2018). *Crown Sky Garden*. Retrieved from https://www.behance.net/gallery/63817071/Crown-Sky-Garden

Monumental Garden of Valsanzibio. (n.d.). *About*. Retrieved from https://www.valsanzibiogiardino.com/about/

National Trust. (n.d.). *The History of Hidcote*. Retrieved from https://www.nationaltrust.org.uk/hidcote/features/the-history-of-hidcote

NC State University, Center for Universal Design. (n.d.). *Sensory Garden*. Retrieved from https://projects.ncsu.edu/ncsu/design/cud/projserv_ps/projects/psexemplars.htm

Osaka Info. (n.d.). *Oizumi Ryokuchi Park*. Retrieved from https://osaka-info.jp/en/page/oizumi-ryokuchi-park

Robinson, M. (2017). The magical gardens of Vansanzibio. *Italy Magazine*. Retrieved from https://www.italymagazine.com/featured-story/magical-gardens-valsanzibio

Roehr, D. (2020). Sense...ible parks and gardens. In M. Rhode, F. Schmidt (Eds.), *Historic Gardens and Society: Culture Nature Responsibility* (pp. 381-389). Germany: Schnell und Steiner.

Shirshekar, S. (2009). *Bagh-e Fin Garden. Asian Historical Architecture*. Retrieved from https://www.orientalarchitecture.com/sid/807/iran/kashan/bagh-e-fin-garden

Taylor, P. (2006). *The Oxford Companion to the Garden*. Oxford: Oxford University Press.

UNESCO World Heritage Centre. (n.d.) *The Persian Garden*. Retrieved from https://whc.unesco.org/en/list/1372

Universal Design Case Studies. (n.d.). *Elizabeth and Nona Evans Restorative Garden*. Retrieved from https://universaldesigncasestudies.org/outdoor-places/parks-gardens/elizabeth-and-nona-evans-restorative-garden

Vaucanson Kelly, A. (2016). *Villandry, or the Art of Garden Design*. Retrieved from https://www.fouracorns.ie/2016/07/10/villandry-the-art-of-garden-design-tout-lart-des-jardins/

Westerkamp, H. (2007). Soundwalking. In A. Carlyle (Ed.), *Autumn Leaves, Sound and the Environment in Artistic Practice* (pp. 49-58). Paris: Double Entendre.

Yamada, T. (2010). A study about changes of the landscape of Katsura Imperial Villa Garden. *Journal of The Japanese Institute of Landscape Architecture, 73*, 367-372. https://doi.org/10.5632/jila.73.367

Yuan, X., Wu, S-X., & Wu, Y. (2012). Soundscape: Theory and praxis in Chinese classical gardens. *The Journal of Acoustical Society of America, 131*(4), 3474-3482. doi: 10.1121/1.4709106

Zhang, Y., Yamaguchi, K. & Kawasaki, M. (2017). A spatial analysis of the pond design to create Okufukasa, a sense of depth: A case study of Katsura Imperial Villa. *Landscape Research, 43*(3), 1-20. doi:10.1080/01426397.2017.1315385

Chapter 4

Becoming Multisensorial

SEE

Sketching is fundamental to our development as designers. It trains us to see and appreciate the details of an existing object, a space, or a building from different views and angles. Sketching teaches us how to analyze the existing environment and to critically see and judge one's own design ideas. This skill is called visual literacy.

"Seeing is a necessary prelude to visual expression" write Norman Crowe and Paul Laseau (Crowe & Laseau, 1984, p. 7), whose prolific book on visual literacy (*Visual Notes for Architects and Designers*, 1984) describes the importance of developing visual literacy. The authors describe visual literacy as: "two skills-visual acuity and visual expression" (Crowe and Laseau, 1984, p. 6). They continue to explain the importance of learning to see, which they call visual acuity, described as: "an intense ability to see information or multiple messages in one's environment with clarity and accuracy" (Crowe and Laseau, 1984, p. 6).

Before we explore different ways of visual sensing and recording, let us first simply consider the verb "sketching." Sketching describes the physical act of putting pen to paper and conveying what one sees in the expanded or detailed sense of seeing. Its physicality, moving your hand along a piece of paper as you visually engage with the object or site in question, is an important aspect to sketching. As Eric Jenkins writes, "sketching in situ is a bodily interaction with the building, site or object...it is necessary to learn from the world by engaging in its reality, its material, volume, its smell, its temperature" (2013, p. 46).

However, what we visually see in front of our eyes and how we interpret the word "visual" will determine if the sketch is either a referential sketch or an analytical sketch. The word "visual" in sketching refers to the two ways that we see with our eyes. The first is to record what can be seen and experienced immediately in front of our eyes, known as referential or representational sketching. The second is to record what cannot be seen immediately in front of our eyes, a process called analytical sketching.

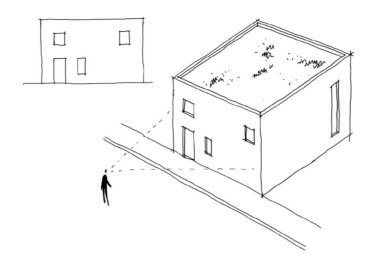

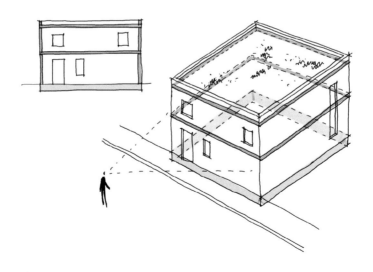

4.1
An analytical sketch of a building (top) vs. a referential sketch, drawn by the author, 2020

There are three classifications of drawing: (1) referential, with a recording function of the past, like a survey; (2) analytical, for example construction details, anticipates the future; (3) design drawings which are a condensation of past and future possibilities (Leatherbarrow, 1998, p. 52). Design drawings are not covered extensively in this book. We are focussed on referential and analytical drawings to practice seeing during recording and analysis.

For example, you are looking at a home that has a façade with five windows, a door, and a pitched roof. A referential sketch would depict what you can see directly before you, so in this instance you would sketch the façade. An analytical sketch however would delve deeper and begin to dissect what is going on beyond the façade. For instance, how might we be able to determine how many floors or rooms the building has? This can only be determined by observing the position of the windows in the façade being in a row or above each other. This observation triggers an analytical thinking process which the brain infers from looking at the façade. Only through the sketcher's trained knowledge of being able to judge the building height and observing the position of the windows above each other, can the observer determine, or rather analyze, if it is a single or double story building. Analytical drawing takes on an anticipatory role, perceiving hidden dynamics like how the interior structure of the building works, or how people might engage with the building.

Before learning analytical sketching, it is recommended to first practice referential sketching. Developing skills in line drawing and recognizing proportions and ratios through referential sketching will train the sketcher's eyes and brain to be more comfortable with analytical sketching. The following exercises practice this.

Throughout the exercises, it is important to engage the other senses beyond the visual, particularly in the analytical sketching process. It is essential to be alert to sound, taste, touch, and smell. Every building, site, and object will embody a myriad of sensorial experiences, and it is our hope that mindfulness is practiced as you work through the exercises highlighted in this book.

A note on hand drawing vs. digital drawing
Research has shown that using tablets "does not compromise" one's ability to learn sketching and hand drawing, and that they in fact provide a space for practicing the same hand-mechanical gestures that would be utilized in paper sketching. In fact, it has been shown that tablets are particularly helpful due to their "mobility and convenience" (Eiliat & Pusca, 2013, p. 135). For example, recording and animating hand drawings is good practice for communicating ideas in studio to a larger audience, or to a client or partner. While we want to encourage students to hand draw in the early stages of design as much as possible, we also recognize the value of technology to ease this process.

4.2
Porsche Street in
Wolfsburg, Germany,
drawn by the author
2004

Referential Sketching

Seeing the environment with our eyes happens intuitively when sketching it. The documentation process that happens during this process helps designers to see and interpret the world around them in a purposeful way. Sketching is an indispensable method for learning to see accurately, and helps develop "visual acuity, which in turn develops visual expression" (Crowe & Laseau, 1984, pp. 6-7). Thus, seeing and sketching are the two ingredients needed for referential sketching.

When becoming a designer, referential sketching is one of the foundational skills which should be acquired in order to develop visual or multisensorial literacy. In the past, artists and designers would be encouraged to travel to new places to develop and practice their drawing and documentation skills through the act of sketching. The Grand Tour was a great example of this, in which European architects and landscape architects were required to travel throughout Europe to sketch landscapes and architecture of great European cities. The architect Michael Graves describes this in his magnificent book *Images of a Grand Tour* (2016), where he reinterprets the Grand Tour in his own journey through Europe in the 1960s.

Referential sketching is learned through continuous practice not only in education but also as a professional. The more you practice, the easier it becomes to look at a space and determine how you might begin to portray it visually. Much in the same way as physical exercise, referential sketching is a process of training your brain to make "the hand and the eye learn to work together" (Jenkins, 2013, p. 28). With more and more practice, it will feel easier and more comfortable for you to focus less on how something will be sketched and more on what will be sketched. As Jenkins writes, "...we can move beyond thinking about sketching to thinking through sketching" (2013, p. 30). Practicing referential sketching will help with analytical sketching later on when sketching becomes an exploratory tool, and later on when sketching helps in developing designs.

Before getting started with exercises it should be noted that the assignments provided here focus on learning and practicing seeing the world around us using the skill of sketching. The initial focus in practicing referential sketching should be on clarity, rather than accracy, this will come later with practice. New sketchers should try not to be inhibited by perfectly representing the scene right away. They should practice loosening up by drawing multiple sketches of the same scene without trying to be too accurate. Readers taking on these assignments should be comfortable and knowledgeable with the following basic drawing skills: orthographic drawing in plan view, sections, elevation, axonometric, isometric, and perspectival drawing. There are many resources available which teach orthographic and perspective drawing (refer to list at the end of this chapter).

Exercise 1: Time to Align

From urban design to landscape architecture to industrial design, drawing decisive and accurate lines is one the most important skills to develop. Whether the sketch is of a tree, a house, or a coffee maker, the line is the foundation of the drawing. Lines are not easy! Lines, while seemingly easy, can be difficult to get right. This first exercise proposes a series of small activities to familiarize yourself with hand drawing and get used to putting pencil to paper.

1. Practice drawing straight lines. Start with one, then five, then 20. Create grids; have them intersect; make them parallel to one another; draw some from an angle. Repeat until you fill a page.

2. As you start to get used to drawing lines, start to give them a story. Choose ten adjectives. Choose ten feelings. If you have one line to draw, how can you convey each word? What does a mysterious line look like? What does a delicious line look like? Repeat until you fill a page.

3. Choose a space near your home, preferably a green or open space. Walk through the space and look around you. Take note of the light, the texture, the colours. Take note of your feelings in the space. Write these down. How might you visually describe what you are seeing? Try to convey your experience using lines—start with how you might convey the space using just one line, then two lines, ten lines, and 20 lines.

4.3 (left)
Line Practice, Marissa Campbell, 2020

4.4
Line Personality, Yaying Zhou, 2020

111

4.5
Line personality,
Wenwen Zhuang,
2020

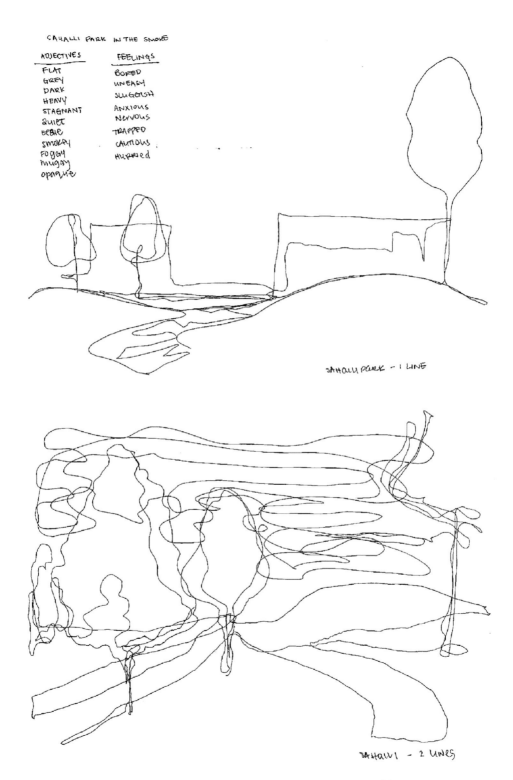

4.6
Sahalli Park in lines,
Marissa Campbell, 2020

4.7
A series of cubes,
Jenna Ratzlaff,
2018

Exercise 2: Adding Dimension

For this next exercise we jump from the first dimension (a line), to dimensions two (a square or circle) and three (a cube or sphere). After having practiced sketching with lines, it is next important to learn to think and draw in the third dimension. This skill is essential as designers explore and design three-dimensionally at all scales.

This exercise trains visual acuity through basic three-dimensional sketching and then applies three-dimensional sketching to see and document urban space. From as basic as a cube to as complex as conveying a built form for example, a church with a bell tower or a concert hall, you will look beyond the single line and start to imagine how lines can convey the third dimension.

1. Draw a basic cube. Imagine where the light would be placed on it. Begin to shade the cube to convey this.

2. Draw many different sized cubes. Draw a series of either axonometric or perspective cubes and have them overlap, intersect with, or hide other cubes. Afterwards, imagine where the light would be and shade accordingly. Repeat until you fill a half of a page.

3. Repeat this exercise with another basic shape of your choice.

4. Examine an object in your home. How would you begin to draw it three-dimensionally? Where does the light hit?

5. Choose a space near your home. How might you start to understand this space through drawing? Start by specifying what you think are the vital components to the space—note the lines, geometries, or shapes that stand out.

6. Try setting your drawing to a timer. Draw the space in 30 seconds, and then one minute, two minutes, five minutes, 15 minutes, and 30 minutes.

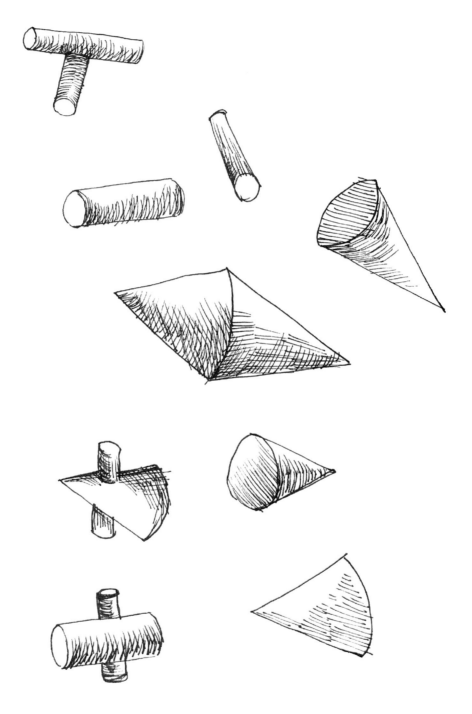

4.8
Basic shape exploration,
Yaying Zhou, 2020

4.9
Simple object in sxpace,
Kathryn Pierre, 2020

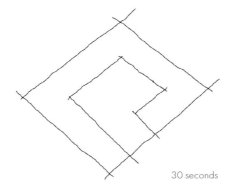
30 seconds

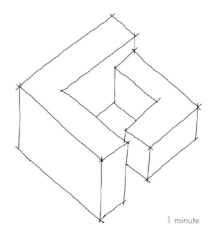
1 minute

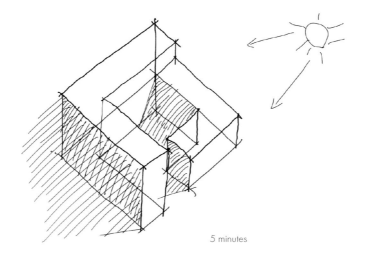
5 minutes

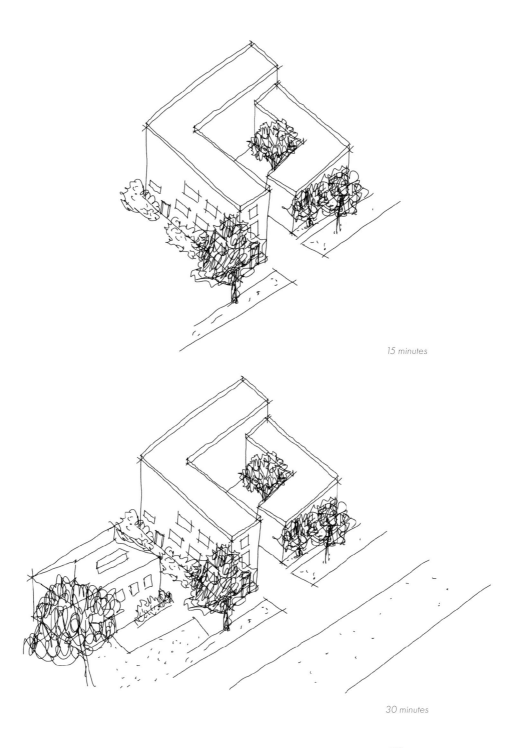

15 minutes

30 minutes

4.10
Timed sketching, Wenwen Zhuang, 2020

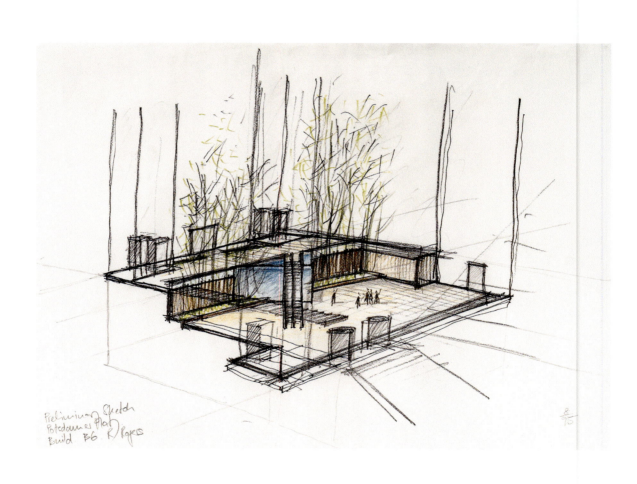

4.11
Space visualized to design landscape by looking at architectural working drawings, drawn by the author, 1995

Analytical Sketching

"...sketching helps us to learn from what is into what may be" (Jenkins, 2013, p. 46).

The previous exercises practiced developing our understanding of how to document what is. In the following sketching exercises, we will move beyond this to examine what may be.

Once you start to feel familiar with referential sketching, analytical sketching is the natural next step. As Crowe and Laseau write, "analytical sketching records what cannot be seen by the camera" (1984, p. 2). These kinds of sketches aim to make the invisible visible. Analytical sketching is essentially like an x-ray machine; it visualizes the bones, muscles, and tendons under the skin and how they function together. In spatial design, analytical sketches can begin to depict anything from how sound hits a wall, to how a wood frame can hold up a building. Like referential sketching, analytical sketching needs to be practiced throughout one's design career. It takes some practice, but once you are able to think and draw spaces analytically, a whole new world opens up.

Analytical sketching requires more deep thinking than referential sketching, and thus even more coordination between the eye and the hand. Seeing analytically must be trained "often in stages" (Jenkins, 2013, p. 39). While a seemingly slow process, sketching in stages will help to develop this skillset in a way that you will eventually enable you to interpret and draw even the most minute of details.

Analytical drawing is a research tool (Have & van den Toorn, 2012, p. 75; Unwin, 2007, p. 102). Drawing is thinking in action; it is a tool for observing, investigating, understanding, and creating. The beauty of a hand sketch versus a photo or a recording is that as the drawer you need to actively participate in the space you are in. The visualized, drawn analysis of what we are engaging with gives us more insight, igniting our imagination and allowing us to begin to think of different ways to engage, problem solve, and design.

The following exercises act as methods for you to begin to understand how to think and draw analytically.

4.12
Analysis of the Beaty
Biodiversity Museum
in Vancouver, Canada,
Mingjia Chen, 2018

Exercise 3: Mapping

"Escaping this flatland is the essential task of envisioning information—for all the interesting worlds (physical, biological, imaginary, human) that we seek to understand are inevitably and happily multivariate in nature. Not flatlands." (Tufte, 1990, p. 12).

This exercise requires us to create maps of different scales and different information. Mapping, while often seen solely in a geographic sense, is a recording tool that allows us to highlight data and information in a spatially coherent way. For instance, an Ordinance Survey map shows what has been surveyed in plan view, like buildings, property lines, fields, ditches, tress, powerlines, etc. To use it analytically, one could begin to interpret and represent underground gas pipes. This would then help to determine where not to position a building, to avoid a gas pipe under the building's foundation, reducing maintenance accessibility and safety concerns. Another example could be reading and analyzing the contours, the gradient of the land, on a map. This kind of analysis would determine the surface rainwater runoff from a site and what plant species could live in the different zones of a sloped site with contours dictating plant species. For instance, the zones at the bottom of the site will have a higher moisture content than those at the top, and therefore allow for plant communities tolerating or needing more water to survive.

A critique that often comes with maps is how they are represented in a way that does not employ dimensionality. Data scientist Edward Tufte discusses this at length, and wonders how can elements of the world around us can be mapped in ways that are more engaging than the conventional plan? In this exercise you are tasked with exploring the world around you and finding phenomena that you would like to analyze and map in a way that expresses dimensionality. You should try to rethink the traditional map in plan-view and develop your own maps to document movement in buildings, a process on a site (in the landscape), or engaging an object's conditions (a machine), thereby trying to sketch at all scales.

1. Choose a space near you that you can return to from time to time, preferably a space that has a lot of activity, and bonus points if there is a good spot for you to sit and observe. This can be anything from a museum, to a concert hall, to your local park. Some of the things that you could begin to observe;
    - The movement of a flower during a day
    - The flow of people in the space
    - The colours of the sky
    - Topography
    - The meadow's relationship to the building
    - The movement of living beings throughout a space
    - How trees or plants move in the wind

    Note that this assignment does not necessarily need to be hand drawn, but it is highly recommended that you start sketching in situ and then try using digital or modelling tools afterwards if you feel called to do so.

4.13
Barnacle clustering at different tides, Marissa Campbell, 2020

4.14
Cloud mapping, Kathryn Pierre, 2020

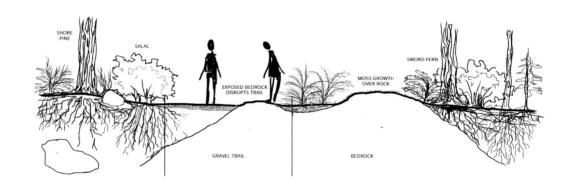

4.15
"What is happening along the Wild Pacific Trail, in and under the forest? The presence of exposed bedrock indicates that the soil depth throughout the forest could be limited, determining what types of plants grow where and how much water they might receive. This section considers how the exposed rock sometimes interrupts the trail system, and usually can only host small species such as mosses and ferns," Marissa Campbell, 2020

Exercise 4: Above, At, and Below Ground

The next exercise prompts you to think about how space functions. In any space, there are a multitude of things happening around you—even if you might not necessarily be able to see them. This exercise entails speculating and analyzing the invisible and seeing the system it is a part of.

1. Choose a space that you can access easily. We recommend looking at a space that spans a block or is generally large in scale, for instance a university campus, a shopping mall, or a commercial street downtown. Begin to break down the space by examining the following scales and their cues;

   - *Above ground*
     - What are the building heights?

     - How do they relate to the trees? To the birds? To the sky?

     - Where does the rain go when it hits the building? Does the building or its landscape do anything to deal with water? How could you describe this in a diagram?

     - Where does the sun reflect? How might that look from the inside? Are there shaded areas?

   - *Ground level*
     - How and where do people move through the space? How do vehicles move through the space?

     - What kind of plants are there, if any? What is their relationship to the street? What is their relationship and scale to your body?

     - Can you interact with the built form? If so, how?

   - *Underground*
     - Imagine the types of systems that may be operating beneath your feet—utilities, water drainage, root systems. How might you convey the intricacies of the invisible underground? How far down do these systems go?

   Note that this assignment does not necessarily need to be hand drawn, but it is highly recommended that you start sketching in situ and then try using digital or modelling tools afterwards if you feel called to do so.

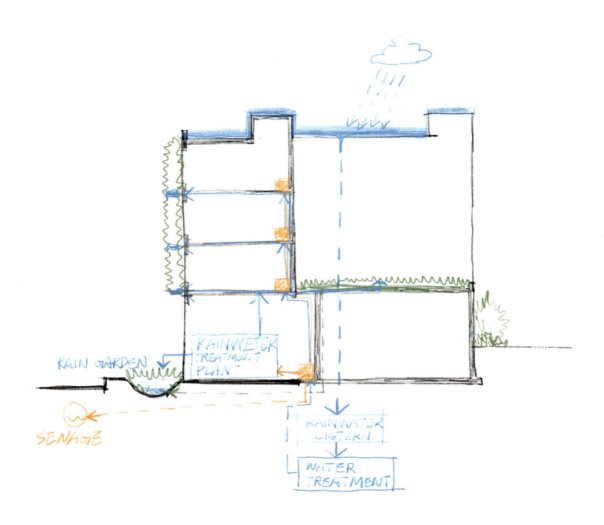

4.16
Examining the flow of water, Wenwen Zhuang, 2020

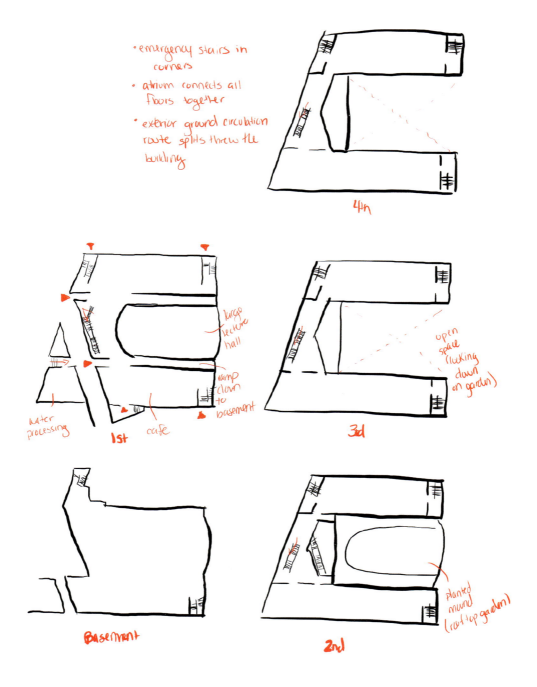

4.17
Analysis of the floor levels of the AMS Building at UBC in Vancouver, Canada, Jenna Ratzlaff, 2018

4.18
Polaroid from a site visit in Orick, California,
Michelle Gagnon-Creeley, 2019

Photography

"Seeing as a way of knowing and photography as a medium of thought" (Whiston Spirn, 2014, p. 114).

Photography serves as a record of the seeing process. The term photography is derived from Greek words *photos*, which means light, and *graphe*, which means to write, resulting in the direct translation "writing of light". The term *graphe* could also be interpreted as a tool or instrument of recording. The world has been constantly recorded through photographs since the camera's invention in 1839, as Susan Sontag wrote, "about everything has been photographed, or so it seems" (1973, p. 1). This inventory has only increased exponentially with digital photography becoming a tool that is easily accessible to anyone, and with free sharing platforms such as Instagram, YouTube, Facebook, and Flickr allowing anyone from around the world to post their work. What would Sontag say today about these digital platforms? In the past, photography was "essentially an act of non-intervention" (Sontag, 1973, p. 8), but digital photography has changed this. Photos are no longer specific documents depicting a specific day, time and light exposure anymore; digital photography has allowed for the possibility of taking more shots as well as having images digitally altered.

Photography is everywhere now, and digitization has made it an instant tool. Images can now be heavily manipulated away from reality with photo-rendering software. Digital tools allow for an even wider range of control in photography. Focus and exposure can be modified instantly just by touching some buttons. With that, one has the ability of even more evidence recording than analog cameras did.

Visual thinking, writes landscape architect and scholar Anne Whiston Spirn, can be learned "through the practice of looking, drawing, photographing, seeking and studying patterns, selecting images and arranging them in series and sequences" (2014, pp. 117-118). In the past, information was mostly recorded by writing, but the distribution of photographic images, first analog and now digital "provides possibilities of recording" (Sontag, 1973, p. 122). As Sontag writes, "photography meant note-taking on potentially everything in the world, from every possible angle" (Sontag, 1973, pp. 137-138). For Spirn, photography is much more than recording—she sees the camera as a thinking tool (2014, p. xi). One of the potentials of photography lies in recording the experience of time and space in an image (Whiston Spirn, 2014, p. 38). For example, early photographs of the Swiss Alps taken in different years from the same position visually document the rapid melting of the glaciers due to climate change. This photographic record inspires visual thinking, as in the synthesis of rising temperature data and visual proof of snow and ice melt, confirming the detrimental ecological impact on the landscape. Without this photographic record, the impact would not be felt quite as dramatically. It is only a series of images such as these that can convey the change that is occurring. While we can write or draw this phenomenon, nothing will compare to, or will have as much of an effect on us as, the photo. Photography is a record of the seeing experience. Whiston Spirn writes "to photograph mindfully, is to look and think, to open a door between what can be seen directly and what is hidden" (2014, p. 113). These seeing and interpreting skills form a language that can be learned and practiced in the same way as we learn a language.

4.19
Landscape types in Haida Gwaii, Canada, Michelle Gagnon-Creeley, 2019

Photography is a visual thinking tool that provides great possibilities to practice visual literacy. Photography is much more accessible today with the advent of technology such as smart phones, aerial photography, and drone technology. More angles and lenses to see with are more available than ever before. Easy access to photographic tools can be used in combination with detailed survey maps (topography, rivers, vegetation, geological). Whiston Spirn explains that through this kind of an analysis we are able to perceive what the space was and could be (2014, p. 117). Photography can be used at all scales, from an object, to a building, to a region. Photographs also serve as a historical record that we can build upon. For instance, recorded evidence of the past is important to conserve a building's design or to develop it for further use. Knowing the use of different building materials in historic buildings or plant species in historic gardens can assist in developing new designs that can reference what exists or could be improved upon. Photography is much more than a recording tool—it initiates visual and critical thinking as the photographer reads the images they create. Whiston Spirn writes, "to see a place in terms the processes that produce them is to read past and future in the present, to distinguish artifacts from portents, and to plan the future wisely" (2014, p. 117).

Walter Benjamin wisely says in his essay *A Short History of Photography*, "the illiterate of the future, will not be the man who cannot read but the one who cannot take a photograph...but must we not also count as illiterate the photographer who cannot read his own pictures?" (1931, p. 25). Photography can only act as a visual thinking tool in design if visual literacy is taught and practiced. While Benjamin wrote this prediction nearly 100 years ago, his warning is just as relevant today. With the dramatic changes that we are seeing in our environments, it is imperative as designers that we become experts at reading and understanding the world around us—our communities depend on it (Whiston Spirn, 2014, p. 117).

The following exercises try to train us to see what is around us and recording it with a camera to begin the visual thinking process.

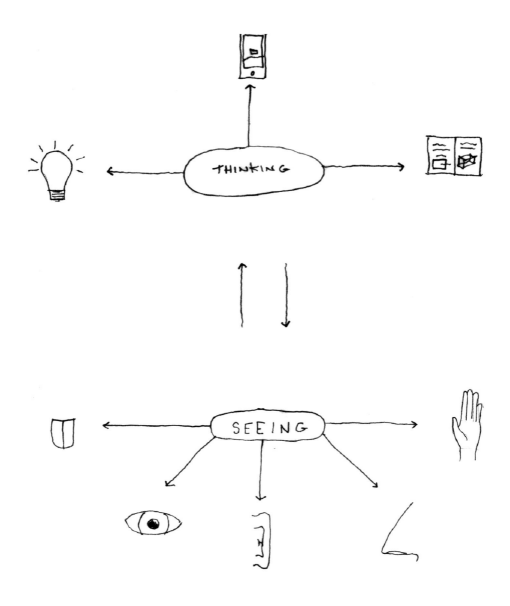

4.20
Exercise summary,
Berend Kessler, 2020

Exercise 5: Seeing > Visual Thinking > Idea

For this exercise you will photograph a series of images that will train your seeing and visual thinking skills to create and visualize your own idea. This exercise can be done at all scales, from an object to a region, however, we recommend starting small first. For this exercise you will need a camera and your sketchbook. It is important that the visual thinking process be annotated.

1. Take a walk in your neighbourhood and observe different plants (such as trees, shrubs, ground cover, etc.) or building details (doors, windows, fences, roofs, stairs). There is no need to photograph your chosen theme just yet.

2. Choose one of these elements that you would like to study deeper. Some examples include: doors, public seating, paving patterns, or fences.

3. When you have chosen your theme, you may use your camera to take images of this element when you see it. Be sure to try different angles to see and study the individual object in detail. Later on, you may even want to look at aerial images depending on the scale of the chosen object.

4. Group similar objects and angles that you have photographed and lay them out side by side to compare (printing your photos or using a table will be easier for the rest of the activity). As an example, if we were looking at doorways, some groupings could be entrance doors with windows, no windows, different shapes and sizes of windows, doors made of wood, or metal, etc. Group them by themes.

    - Can you recognize similar patterns? For example, different positions of the windows in entrance doors or different door handles and keyholes?

    - Can you recognize different forms? For example, window form with or without glazing bars, and what forms have the glazing bars?

5. Annotate or sketch on the poster using tracing paper or your tablet if you recognize similarities. Try to account the decision of your chosen series by annotating. Don't be afraid to take notes on this assignment! Develop reasons why these patterns are happening or as Whiston Spirn describes it "plot a line of reasoning" (2014, p. 46).

6. Repattern! Now try to reinterpret your chosen object, based on the patterns or differences you recognized. Combine the details in the images to develop and express new ideas. This new idea can be represented by annotated hand drawings and diagrams or collaged digitally.

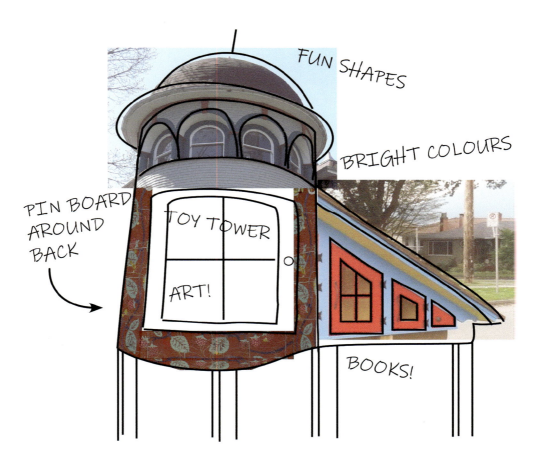

4.21
An analysis of neighbourhood book exchanges and a proposed new structure, Yette Gram, 2020

Visual Analysis - Neighbourhood Book Exchanges

NEIGHBOURHOOD BOOK EXCHANGE PRECEDENTS

ROOFLINE STUDY

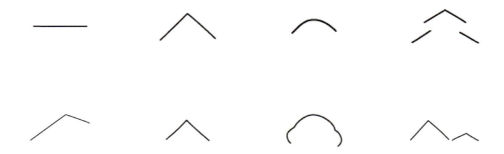

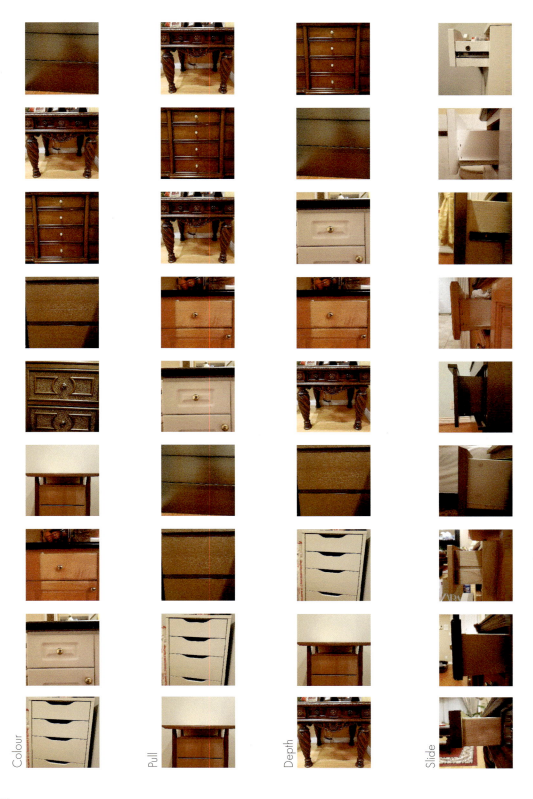

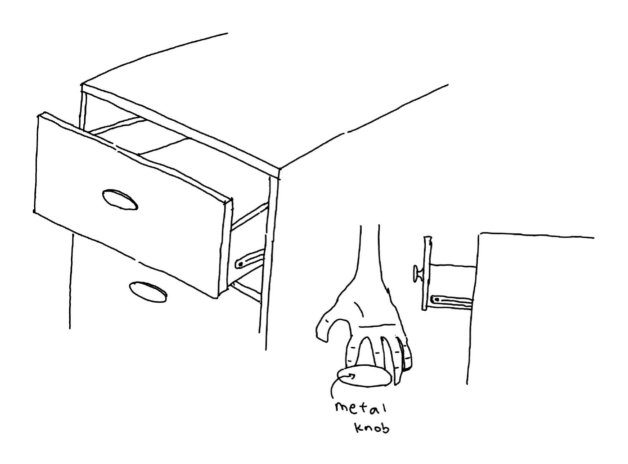

4.22
An analysis of drawers, and a proposed new cabinet, Vicky Cen, 2020

Exercise 6: Time Stamp

This exercise looks at the element of time, and how we might produce a series of photographs to depict how something changes over a day, a week, a season, or a year.

1. Take a walk in your neighbourhood, preferably somewhere close enough to you that you can engage with the chosen object or site multiple times.

2. Choose an object or site that you would like to observe over time and think about the time intervals for which you would like to set. For instance, how a plant might change in the span of a day or a week, how the seasons affect a certain site, or how and where people interact with a space on a weekday.

3. Take photos of the same thing over your previously decided time interval. Annotate these photos. What are you noticing? What has changed? What has not changed?

4.23 (left)
The evolution of a sunrise,
Michelle Gagnon-Creeley,
2020

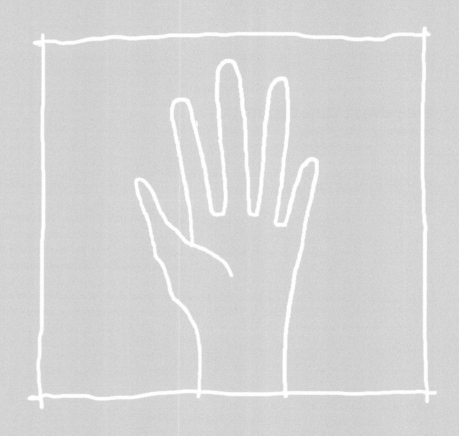

TOUCH

Touch drives design; the skin and its relationship to space is the most important sense to be explored in the design process. Touch, Pallasmaa writes, is "the mother of all senses...the parent of our eyes, ears, nose and mouth...it is the sense which became differentiated into the others" (2005, p. 11). In the animal kingdom, touch is the most primal sense used, from protection to finding food. In fact, many animals' non-visual sensorial abilities are far more refined than our own. While touch might not be seen to be as vital to us, touch plays an important role in a human's physical and mental wellbeing (Ackerman, 1990, pp. 94-95). Like other animals, touch is our most primal sense. As babies, our first sensorial explorations are through touch. This emphasizes that the skin is the first way that we start to see-skin is seeing physically.

It is important to understand that buildings, landscapes, and objects are not experienced solely as "a series of isolated retinal pictures, but in its fully integrated material, embodied and spiritual essence" (Pallasmaa, 2005, p. 12). Since the Renaissance, the visual experience has been placed as the sense of most importance while touch was considered the least important (Pallasmaa, 2005, pp. 15-16). The invention of the one-point perspective during the Renaissance made the eye the focal point of how we see and interpret the world before us, and we continue to work primarily from this perspective today (Pallasmaa, 2005, p. 16). During the Renaissance, the eye was the dominant organ in designing cities and buildings, with cities like Sabbioneta, Italy being designed to please the eye from a central point of view. Due to this hierarchy of the visual sense, modernism and most contemporary Western architecture and design have neglected the body and the other senses (Pallasmaa, 2005, p. 17). Vision tends to operate automatically and "supplant touch as the dominant sense" (Landau, 2018, p. 177). It is worth noting however that non-Western architecture has not necessarily followed this approach, with Pallasmaa noting that "indigenous clay and mud architecture...seem to be born of the muscular and haptic senses more than the eye" (2005, p. 26). Western architecture has also had some notable deviations to more touch-oriented design and included "a multitude of sensory experiences" in their buildings by such architects as Frank Lloyd Wright, Alvar Alto, Steven Holl, Peter Zumthor, and Glen Murcutt (Pallasmaa, 2005, p. 70).

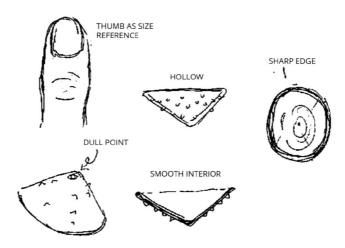

DRAWING BY OTHER SENSES

 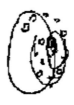 

BLINDFOLDED DRAWING

DRAWING WITH SIGHT

4.24
Understanding a seashelll through touch, Marissa Campbell, 2020

To design with touch in mind is more important now than ever before. Our dependence on our phones has created a society disconnected from tactile experiences outside of our devices. Designers should take on the responsibility of inclusive design. Visually impaired individuals are often excluded in the visual experience, but we can avoid this if we focus our design on touch along with the other senses. What might be the lessons or designs that come forth when we work with blindfolds? As we increasingly use devices with touch screens our skin becomes much more than "exterior skin" (Lupton, 2018a, p. 38). Our fingers are now capable of instantly accessing, gaining, and manipulating information; "we now touch information itself: we stretch, crumple, drag, flick it aside…the illusion of direct interaction changes the way we experience the digital world" (Lupton, 2018a, p. 41).

How a space feels to our bodies is arguably the most important consideration in design. A bench that is made of stone or of wood will feel different to our bodies. As Catherine Dee writes, "wet and dry stone smell different…and stone reflects sound; clatters with hard shoe soles, while earth muffles it". (2001, p. 199). Materiality is the gateway for creating the ambience of a space, for evoking physical and emotional feelings, for touching the soul. While the focus on materiality often goes to manmade materials, plant life is also extremely important to consider. Walking barefoot on grass is a very different experience from walking barefoot on asphalt. We know these things unconsciously, however, the following exercises will begin to make you start to interpret the world before you without using your eyes. This is where you need to start to listen and be mindful of your body and how it moves and feels space.

4.25
An exploration of the feeling of a
random object, Valia Puente, 2018

Exercise 7: Using our hands

The first assignment will have you rely on the body part that is most familiar with touch—your hands.

1. Have someone fill a box with objects for you; you should be unaware of what the box is filled with.

2. Closing your eyes or wearing a blindfold, choose an unidentified object from the box.

3. Feel the object. Rather than trying to determine what the object is, focus on how it feels in your hand.

4. Try to draw the object. Some prompts as you draw:
    - What does the object feel like?
        - Is it hot or cold?
        - Is it smooth, gritty, hard, soft, rubbery, etc.?
        - Does the material of the object feel familiar?

    - Does the object feel comfortable in your hand? Where do your fingers fall? How does it fit in your palm?

    - How can you convey the feeling of it? If you are stuck on this, write down words that you would use to describe the feeling. If you were to illustrate these words, what would that look like?

5. Try to repeat this exercise without the blindfold. Are there differences or similarities in how you treat and feel the object?

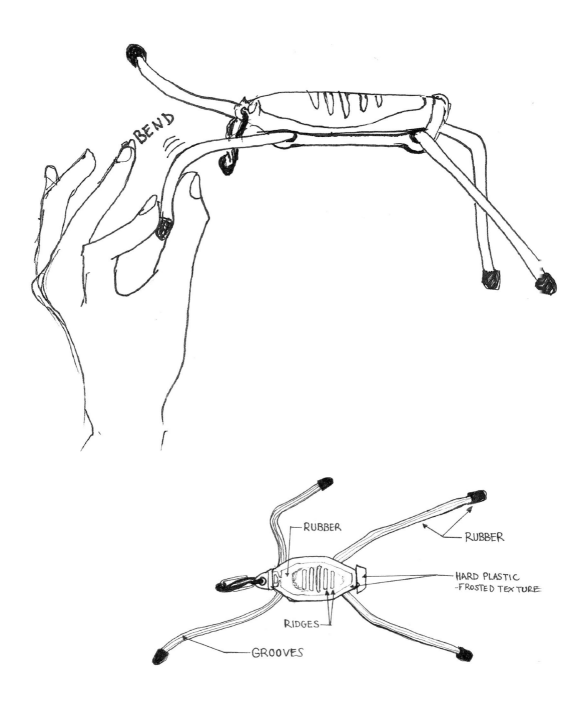

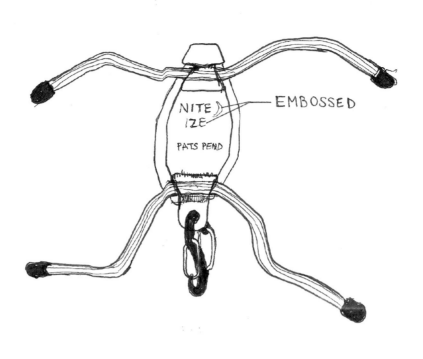
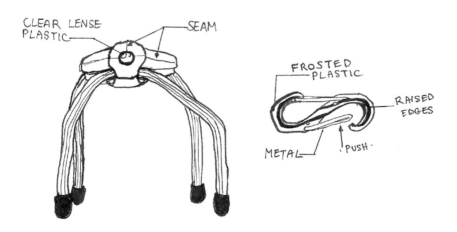

4.26
An exploration of a bug light,
Jennifer Reid, 2020

4.27
The re-creation of a tactile experience of an unknown object, Mingjia Chen, 2018

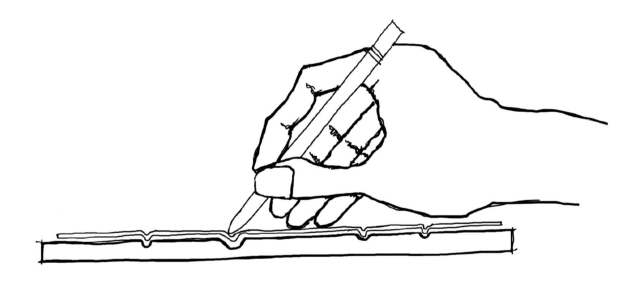

4.28
Drawing on a tactile board, adapted from *The Senses: Design Beyond Vision*, drawn by the author, 2020

153

Exercise 8: Drawn to Touch

This exercise is inspired by Steven Landau's "Drawing by Touching" chapter in *The Senses: Design beyond Vision*. Landau describes how visually impaired artists draw using "tactile drawing boards" that are made with a soft rubber mat placed under a sheet of paper. Applying pressure with a pen, this mat creates depressed furrows in the paper which can be felt by one of the drawer's hands while the other hand draws the image (Landau, 2018, p. 177). Firm pressure on the pen creates deeper raised furrows in the paper, which expresses thicker and darker lines while soft pressure creates lower raised furrows in the paper expressing thinner and grey lines (Landau, 2018, p. 177). Through touch, the artist can then express themselves through drawing (Landau, 2018, p. 177).

This whole drawing experience is vital to facilitate drawing inclusion of the visually impaired and it stimulates the tactile experience to include touch intentionally in the observation and design process of buildings, site, and objects.

In this exercise you will need to buy a couple of rubber pads a bit larger than the paper sizes you anticipate using with varying types of softness and resilience. We recommend different types of hardness so that the pressure while drawing will create different textures.

1. Set up your tactile board, placing your mat underneath your paper. Blindfold yourself. Similar to the previous exercise, we want you to learn to draw without visual perception. Leave the blindfold on for the whole exercise session, so the brain does not revert immediately back to visual mode.

2. Try to draw lines on the board, press softly first and then harder to draw thin and thick and then thin. Feel the lines you have just drawn and do not remove the blindfold.

3. After you feel comfortable drawing lines and other doodles, imagine an object, a tree, a chair, or a person and draw them on the board. Feel the result. If you feel confident draw something more complex like a building or a path in the landscape. Most important do not remove the blindfold until you are done.

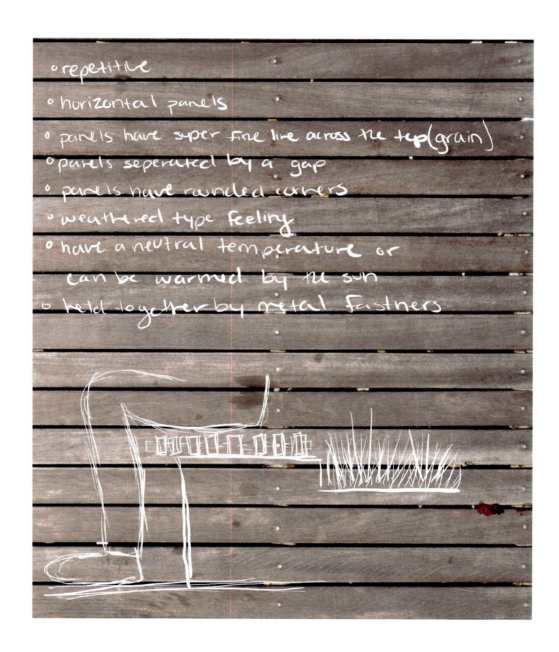

deck | wood bench

Exercise 9: Tactile Body Space

In the first exercise we focused on how we might convey the tactile experience of an object, or how a substance might feel in our hands. In this exercise we will start to look at the tactile experience from a larger scale. This exercise will be a little more complex, in which we will examine what it feels like to be in space.

1. Choose a space where you can sit for about an hour—this can be anywhere, from your home, a café, a church, a university campus.

2. Start by simply sitting or standing in the space. Close your eyes and listen. Open them and scan what is in your direct environment.

3. Begin to engage with the materials that are present. What material are the doors, the walls, the furniture, the floors? How do these make you feel?

4. Try to convey how this space feels using words—is it smooth, gritty, hard, soft, rubbery, etc.? Simply record what you notice and how you feel in terms of light, sound, patterns, textures, colour, temperature, smell. Try to illustrate the texture and feeling of the spaces or materials that are popping out to you.

5. Do these feelings you are noticing relate to the materials? Is there something that feels cozy or cold? Why does it feel that way?

Sketch parts of the space that feel most relevant in describing the material sensations of being there. These sketches can be diagrams, mappings, orthographic drawings, or material collages. You can also use the video and sound recording device on your smart phone to create tactile recordings or animated videos explaining your tactile experiences.

4.29 (left)
Annotated sketch of a wood bench, Jenna Ratzlaff, 2018

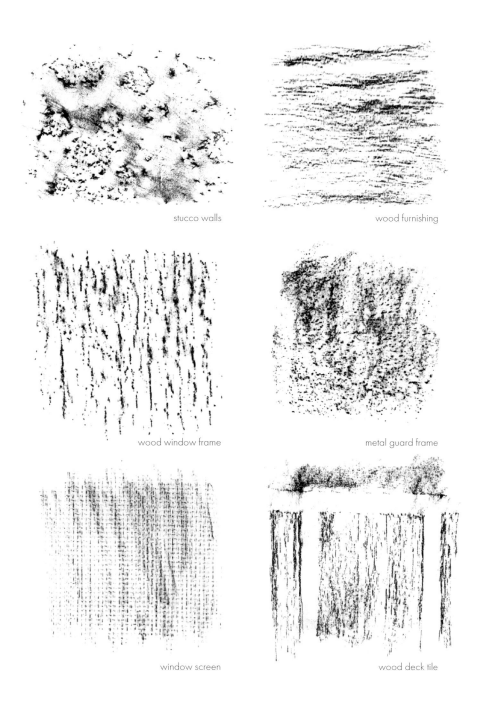

4.30
Exploration of the tactile experiences of a patio, Marissa Campbell, 2020

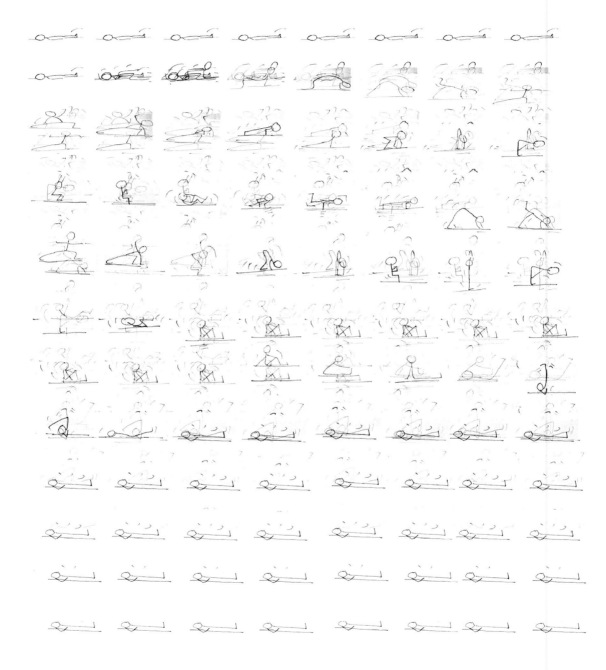

4.31
Mapping movement through a yoga practice, Josh Fender, 2020

Exercise 10: Movement

Our bodies continuously engage with the spaces that we exist in. In this exercise we will be examining the movements that our bodies go through as they engage in space. Choose a room, hallway, or outdoor space and begin to consciously evaluate your body's interactions with your chosen space.

Take, for example, the following scenario of a staircase. Consider the following questions as your body engages with it:

- How do your feet touch the ground?

- Is there a pattern to the number of steps taken at a time? Do you skip steps or take each step?

- How do your legs move as you take one step at a time vs. multiple steps at a time? How does the rest of your body move?

- How does the railing feel? How do you hold the railing? Do you extend your arm or are you close to the railing?

- If you were to sit on a step, is it comfortable? Do you extend your legs or have them at a 90° angle?

- If you were to notate the steps you take in plan view, what would that look like?

4.32
Mapping the dynamic experience of stairs, Vicky Cen, 2020

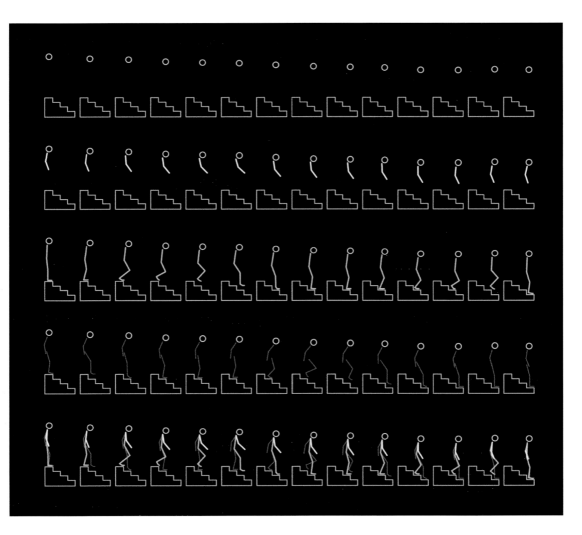

4.33
An examination of the body's kinesthetic relationship to stairs, Fabian Lobmueller, 2018

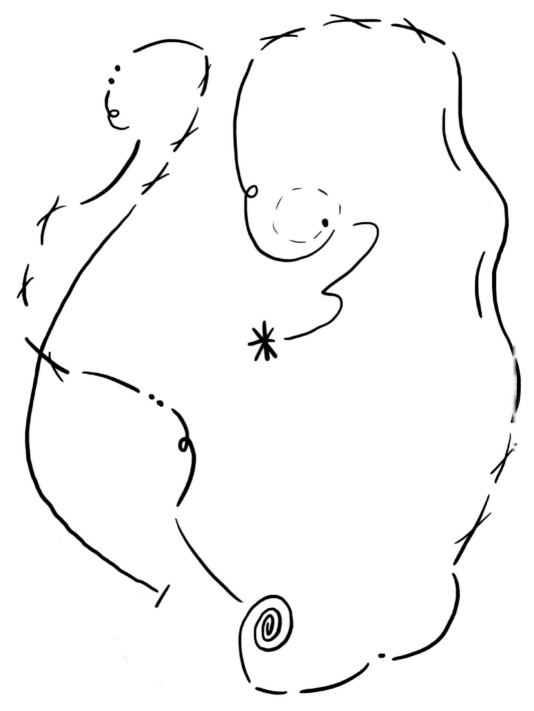

4.34
Notation of a figure skating routine, Michelle Gagnon-Creeley, 2020

Exercise 11: Footwork
"Dance has been called moving architecture..." (Hutchinson Guest, 1990, p. 203)

Dancers and figure skaters annotate their choreography on paper in ways that are visually beautiful and spatially aware. They are maps in their own right, recording graphically how and where the body and feet should be—where one should travel to, how one should place their feet, what kind of movement is taking place. In this exercise we would like you to try and map where and how you move in a space and interpret that on paper.

1. Find an open space where you can move around or dance, preferably a park or an open space.

2. Move through the space—walk, run, skip, dance, let your body move freely. Feel free to listen to music while you do this!

3. Record where and how you moved. Some prompts:
   - Can you map where you moved? What does this look like in plan view? Where did you travel?
   - How do you distinguish a step from a swirl? A hop from a skip? What does a pause look like?
   - Let's examine this three-dimensionally, how might this look like from an axonometric view?

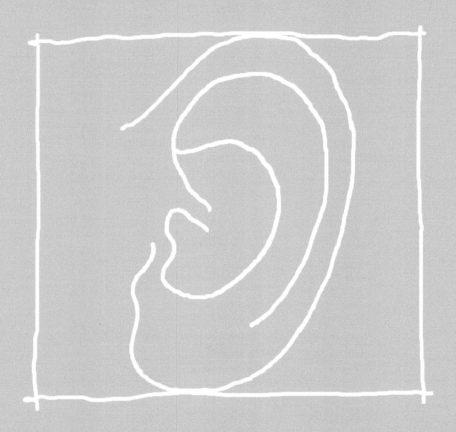

HEAR

"Architecture shapes sound–and sound shapes architecture" (Lupton, 2018a, p. 49).

Imagine sitting in a café or on a busy bus. Close your eyes and listen. Without seeing, can you visualize what the space might look like in your mind? Vibrations guide our ears much like how light guides our eyes.

"Sound transforms what we see" (Mau, 2018, p. 23); an echo can measure distance in space, and the vibrations of music can affect the skin to the point of giving us goosebumps. These vibrations engage with our bodies in ways that can conjure vivid emotional or psychological responses. Much like smell, sound is complex and happens all around us, affecting how we unconsciously experience space.

Music is often the first thing to come to mind when we consider sound, and it is something that should be considered as a designer. Oliver Sacks writes in his book *Musicophilia*, "for virtually all of us, music has a great power, whether or not we seek it out or think of ourselves as particularly musical" (2007, pp. x-xi). Music can affect us in many ways. At times it acts like our diary or our journal, or as the backdrop to a good conversation, or as our motivation during strenuous times. It can recall memories of a specific time or place. Music has a way of "engraving" itself on the brain (Sacks, 2007, p. xii). Music is also a physical process—as Nietzsche observes "we listen to music with our muscles...not just auditory and emotionally" (as quoted in Sachs, 2007, p. xii). Music, like sound, touches the skin through the sound waves deflected in space, the walls, the floor, the roof, the plants, and through the air. Unlike atmospheric sound, music is multi-faceted, stimulating not only our ears but also our minds, triggering "sensory channels that make us think and feel, listen and touch, see and imagine" (Bourbounne, 2018, p. 154). For people who are hard of hearing, music is oftentimes absorbed via vibrations on the skin by touching a speaker as it plays music (Bourbonne, 2018, p. 153).

Sound often borrows from the other senses, especially when describing it—for instance using the words "sharp" or "soft" to describe sound also conjure a physical and tactile meanings (Copeland, 2017, p. 1). Music and sound have a tendency to evoke certain feelings or visualizations once the vibrations hit the ear. Research over the past two decades suggests that music could also have connections to other senses. Otherwise known as synesthesia, it is a phenomenon that occurs when one sense relates to another (Copeland, 2017). For instance, seeing colour or shape while listening to a song or experiencing a certain flavour when listening to specific type of music is a type of synesthesia. While there are still a lot of discoveries to be made, it provides interesting insight into how the senses can relate to one another and affect a person's perception of space. As Ellen Lupton writes, "studying sound through visual or tactile means is a powerful method of invention" (Lupton, 2018c, p. 216). For instance, designer Guy Featherstone graphically integrates sound into a multisensorial experience (Lupton, 2018c, p. 212). When creating music covers for Diagonal Records, Featherstone considers it important to design for the experience of listening to the music, not only the sound. In order to visualize the "sonic terrain" he asks questions like "What does the sound feel like? What does it look like? What is the experience?" (Lupton, 2018c, p. 212). We can also see this when looking at jazz album covers from the 1960s, as they are often a graphic and physical interpretation of what we are hearing (Lupton, 2018c, p. 216). This type of imagery "offers a rich path for experiencing sound beyond the audible" (Lupton, 2018c, p. 216). This multi-layered questioning has also been explored physically with the human body. Copeland describes full sensory dancing experiments at the Smithsonian, in which participants were blindfolded and music had to felt through smell, taste, and touch (Copeland, 2017).

On a primitive level, humans use sound to measure distance; it has been used for centuries as an orientation tool. The echo of a captain's whistle against a rocky coastline deflected sharper sounds while a sandy beach created a softer sound (Westerkamp, 2007, p. 55). Indigenous communities use hearing as a tool for hunting, interpreting the health of plants and the forest, and for navigation. As a designer, understanding sound in space—in particular how acoustic stimuli function and are experienced in a space is essential to design. As Pallasmaa writes "hearing structures articulates the experience and understanding of space" (Pallasmaa, 2005, p. 49). Every space—indoor or outdoor, urban or rural has its own multi-layered sound experience that enhances the overall dwelling experience. These experiences are heavily influenced by the materials used within the space—as each object or material will create unique sounds when interacted with. To learn how to listen to the sounds of plants, rocks, wood, or metal in relation to our bodies is important for us to begin to understand how we design spaces for comfort, work, pleasure, or rest. Attentive listening thus should be trained continually during one's design career.

The city can often sound and feel like a whirlwind—as people have conversations with one another; cars drive by; shop doors open and close, and the leaves of street trees rustle in the wind. City life reverberates onto the buildings and street, and depending on the materials of said structures, the sounds will be experienced differently (Pallasmaa, 2005, p. 51). Listening to the sounds in a historic European city with its narrow streets and stone or brick buildings creates a completely different soundscape from a modern city such as Los Angeles with its wide freeways. Historic parks with old tree growth sound different from the High Line in New York. Sound has to be considered and designed for different contexts, such as for buildings which are static, or for a site, a park or garden, which is in constant change due to growth.

It was Raymond Murray Schafer who established the phrase soundscapes (Adams et al., 2007, p. 1) and introduced soundwalks in the early 1970s (Henshaw, 2014, p. 42). Soundwalks were an attempt to heighten the sensory experience in the environment intentionally, by limiting a sense such as sight to experience sound more deeply. Since then, research has been carried out to understand soundscapes through sound-walking. Current research recognizes sounds can be a positive contribution to space and are not always detrimental. Thus, sound can be a concept driver for environmental planning, landscape architecture, and architecture (Adams et al., 2007, p. 4). Recent research by Gunnar Cerwén et al. summarizes existing environmental design soundscape research and proposes "soundscape actions"; a series of tools for developing sound design concepts for the urban environment (2017).

As designers it is important that while we visit sites, we sit, listen, and absorb the multitude of sounds that reach our ears. Pallasmaa reminds us that we often are not attuned to the subtleties of sound in our everyday lives, writing "...we are not normally aware of the significance of hearing spatial experiences, although sound often provides the temporal continuum in which visual impressions are embedded" (Pallasmaa, 2005, p. 49). A movie without sound loses its plasticity or three-dimensionality; silent movies therefore had to exaggerate their physical expressions to compensate for the absence of sound (Pallasmaa, 2005, p. 49). Sound is everywhere and "omni-directional" while vision is "directional"—sound surrounds and envelops us entirely in a way that the visual cannot (Pallasmaa, 2005, p. 49). This makes sound far more complex to document and design for.

The following exercises challenge and broaden your hearing and listening abilities to heighten your listening skills so you can begin to understand and depict your own soundscapes.

Exercise 12: Tuning In
This exercise references the work of Westerkamp's soundscapes. The goal is for you to begin to understand the world purely through its sounds.

1. Choose a space in your neighbourhood to analyze. This could be a large garden or park in your neighbourhood with a path system and multiple spaces to visit, a bridge or a neighbourhood block.

2. Begin by finding a space to stand or sit and close your eyes. Start listening. Keep note of the sounds you are experiencing—either in writing, drawing, or an audio recording.

3. Some prompts as you tune in:

    - What do you hear? What do you visualize when hearing these sounds?

    - Does your body make any sounds? Can you move without making sound? Is it possible?

    - Is there a feeling or memory that you can associate to the sound(s) you are hearing?

    - Could you attribute a colour or texture to the sound(s)?

    - If the sound was a physical object, what would that object look like?

    - What are the sources of the different sounds?

    - Can you detect interesting patterns, rhythms, or beats?

This exercise does not necessarily need to be hand drawn-digital or modelling tools can also be used.

4.35
Sound analysis of the High Line, Kemeng Gao, 2018

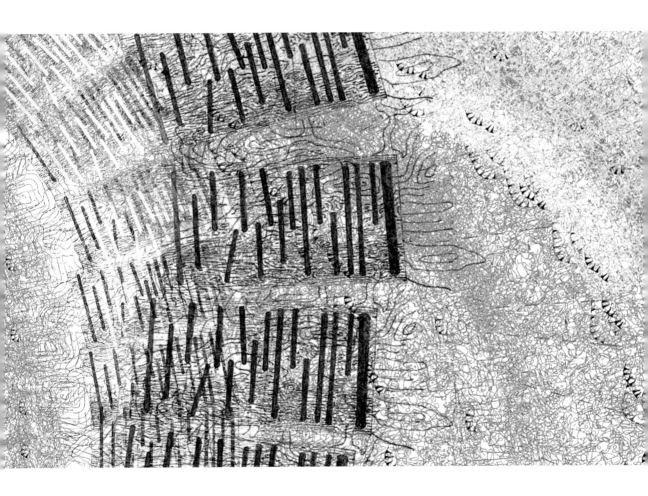

4.36
Sound analysis, of
Heather Park in
Vancouver, Canada,
Jacob Darowski, 2020

172

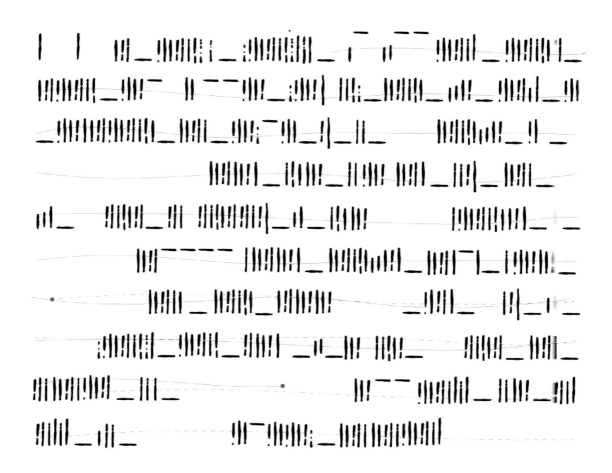

4.37
Sound of typing on a keyboard depicted through time, communication, and muscle memory, the blue line represents background noise, Marissa Campbell, 2020

4.38
Acoustic impression of sounds heard from a balcony, Doug Craig, 2020

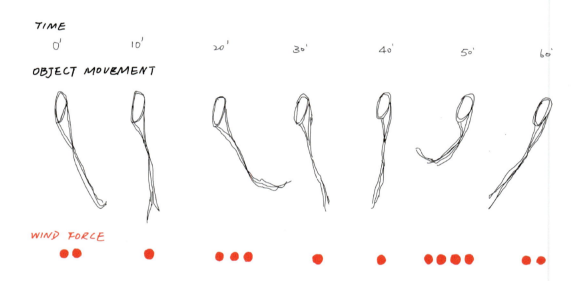

4.39
An analysis of a shoelace in the wind, Wenwen Zhuang, 2020

Exercise 13: Wind Play

Westerkamp's text describes how the sound of wind is everywhere; "voices in old myths, in novels, in poetry, in fairytales and in horror stories" (2007, p. 49). As an exercise, Westerkamp suggests that we "concentrate on one outstanding continuous sound (church bells, motorboat, highway, outdoor music) and listen to the acoustic game the wind plays with it" (Westerkamp, 2007, p. 49). Outdoor sound is carried by even the slightest amount of wind and has immediate impact on nearby listeners. For instance, a highway or airport sound will be heard more intensely depending on the wind's direction in relation to the position of the listener. Wind plays a key role when analyzing and designing sound in urban and rural areas.

In this exercise you should build an object with which the wind can play, to explore how its direction and intensity impacts the object's movement and acoustical sound interacts within the object. This object can move or can be fixed, but it must display the wind direction and create a sound. Its sound should try to entice observers to notice its presence and it should, if possible, improve the acoustic environment. Some prompts:

- Research windmills, wind sculptures, and light structures made with light material like paper. Study light materials such as Japanese paper and bamboo, or feathers. The search for the construction material should be guided by the wind's physical properties of pressure and intensity.

- Make the object and place it in a space where it can interact with wind.

- Record its movement or its sounds or the relationship between them in the wind either through sketching or digital means.

Love & Death, Ebo Taylor

September, Earth, Wind & Fire

4.40
Visualizing songs, Michelle Gagnon-Creeley, 2020

Exercise 14: Album Art

Inspired by the jazz albums from the 1960s, as mentioned above, this assignment encourages students to create an album cover or an image that best depicts a song.

1. Choose a song. This can be your favourite song, a friend's favourite song, a musical genre you have never listened to. Listen to the chosen song. Close your eyes; immerse yourself. Repeat this step as many times as you need.

2. Begin to draw or write out some experiences from the song. Some prompts:

    - How does the music make you feel emotionally?

    - How does the music make you feel physically? Did you dance? Did you feel a weight on your shoulders?

    - Do any memories or stories come to mind?

    - Do you see or feel any colours?

    - If you had to give the song a shape what would it look like?

    - If you could only use one continuous line, could you describe the song?

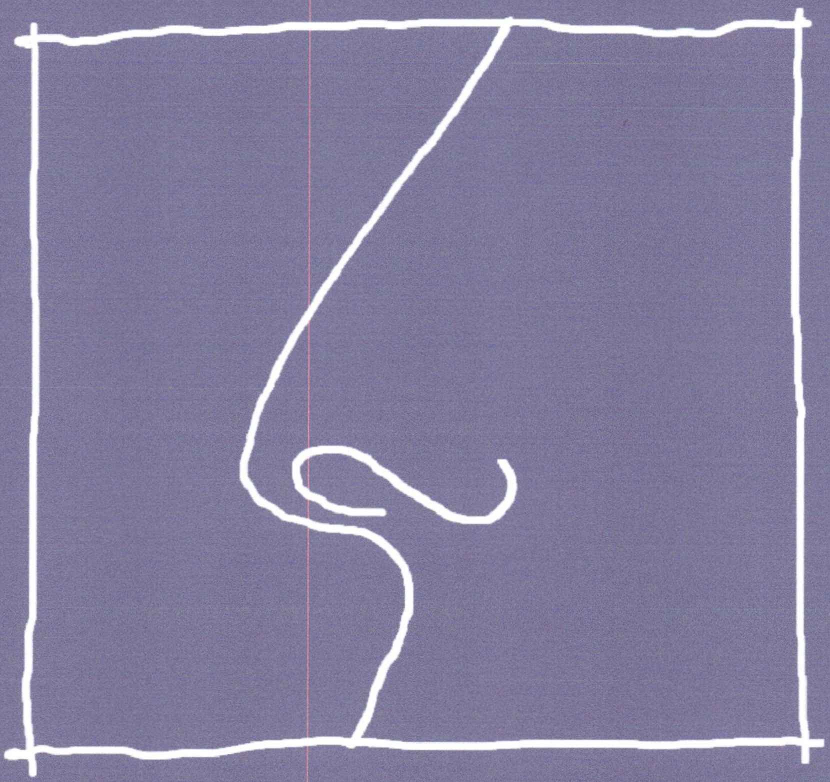

SMELL

Smell cannot be described easily in words; it is intimate and it constantly surrounds us. And yet while it envelops us, it is rarely a part of design discourse. Why is this so? There is speculation that it might perhaps be because it is still seen as an unconventional subject. Andrea Lipps writes, "smell is deeply personal" (2018b, p. 111), whereas a good smell for one person might be repulsive to another, and this may be why designers tend to overlook its importance in spatial design. Another consideration is that our sense of smell is often "muted" (Ackerman, 1990, p. 6). Of all the senses, smell goes unrecognized perhaps because there is no physical way to engage with it in the same way we do with our mouths to taste or fingers to touch. Also smells mix, linger, and disappear in a way that the other senses don't. It makes it difficult to pinpoint their origins (without practice, at least). But while it is seldomly discussed, smell is nonetheless integral to our spatial and contextual experience.

Take for instance how smell guided us in prehistoric times; sweet smells alerted our ancestors when fruit was ripe for consumption; musty smells communicated the need to seek cover from approaching storms. As Lipps notes, "smell has been long the key to survival" (2018b, p. 110). Since early evolution, smell has been integral to our survival and livelihood. Along with touch, smell is seen as a "primal sense" (Lipps, 2018b, p. 109). While it may be hard to understand how our sense of smell today relates to prehistoric times, think back to your childhood home—are there certain smells from then that you can still recall? The smell of freshly washed sheets, the smell of your father's rosebush that he so delicately pruned, the smell of cookies baking in the oven. Smell experiences from childhood can be locked in one's brain for a lifetime and can come surging back as though no time has passed. Many writers and researchers agree that smell is the most memorable sense (Ackerman, 1990, p. 5; Pallasmaa, 2005, p. 54; Lipps, 2018b, p. 113). Smell affects space. "Every dwelling has its individual smell of home" writes Pallasmaa (2005, p. 54).

How we perceive and design for smell varies from culture to culture. In Western culture, smell (and to a certain extent taste and touch) is considered to be private or taboo and often goes undiscussed, as we tend to associate the concept of smells with unpleasant ones like rotten food, body odour or sewers. With vision being the highest sense in the Renaissance-constructed hierarchy, smell was seen as inferior due to its "animalistic" characteristics" (Henshaw, 2018, p. 163). This hierarchical view on smell persists today, whereas "modern Western architecture has largely removed olfactory experiences in the built environment" (Lipps, 2018b, p. 113). Modern office buildings are environmentally controlled, with elaborate systems in place to remove smell, humidity, and temperature fluctuations, leaving little room for olfactory experiences. This contrasts greatly with how other cultures; particularly Indigenous and Eastern cultures place great importance on smell to communicate and understand the world around them. For instance, in Japan ofuro bathtubs are traditionally made out of Hinoki, and this material is chosen for its clean, citrus smell (which resembles that of cedar wood) and for antiseptic purposes (Lipps, 2018b, p. 113). Asian villages and shopping streets are delightful and intentional smellscapes—the odour of walking through a market can be a feast for the nose that heightens the overall visiting or shopping experience in a way that the eyes or ears cannot.

Olfactory experiences are part of design but are often not consciously considered. Whether we are aware of it or not, smell impacts how we build our urban environments. The materials we often use in architecture and interior design like glass, steel, and stone do not smell, making the smell experience in our interior environments limited (Ackerman, 1990, p. 13). However, in landscape architecture this is different. "Before something can be smelled, it has to be airborne" writes Ackerman (1990, p. 13). Building materials in the open space react with rainwater and fluctuating temperatures, releasing molecules into the air, which can then be picked up by our olfactory receptors. Of course, this also occurs with plant materials. The designer selects many plant species specifically for their flowers on the basis of their individual smell, form, and colour. Patrick Mooney examines this in his book *Planting Design, Connecting People and Place* (2019). Mooney describes how the strategy of "being away," from the origin of one's mental fatigue, and placed into a fragrant planted space at designed accessible locations, can reinforce reflection and provide mental restoration (Mooney, 2019, p. 59).

In an urban and rural context, smell can help us remember what the eyes cannot see (Pallasmaa, 2005, p. 54). Smell enhances our imagination, stimulating learning and retention (Ackerman, 1990, p. 11). Smell is often related to a dirty, unclean environment, but in fact smell is part of experiencing a city. You have not seen a city if you have not smelled it: "every city has its spectrum of tastes and odours" writes Pallasmaa (2005, p. 55). If one sees a bakery, the smells that come from it might encourage us to imagine sweet flavours and comfort, or the smells of a fishing town help us imagine a fusing of the sea and land (Pallasmaa, 2005, p. 54). Smell heightens the experience of places and ingrains memories of them in our minds. Pallasmaa refers to this as "a space of smell" (2005, p. 48).

While it has been established in scholarly circles that smell is a vital component to how we design a space, we seldom see this as an important consideration when we actually design. Incorporating or considering smell is not taught intentionally in design schools. Is it because design schools are so focused on theory these days that such subjective and temporal elements are forgotten? This is strange, because smell is around us all the time and has always been. Can it be included more in design pedagogy? Further, how can we teach budding designers to analyze, describe, and depict a sense that is invisible and atmospheric?

Describing smell is difficult. Even in writing, describing smell can be a "real test" (Ackermann, 1990, p. 18). The same could be said for designers. How do you visualize something that is invisible? If you cannot visualize, appreciate, and design for smell, how can you design a space or an object that incorporates smell? How can we visualize space to include olfactory experiences in the design process? It might first be useful to examine how smell is described in words. For instance, Lipps writes how we tend to describe smell in two ways, we either "reference its source-cut grass, or a physical property-effervescent" (2018a, 110). If smell is described mostly by its qualities and our personal experiences with them, as designers we could perhaps take advantage of its spatial qualities and begin to describe smells visually through a tool such as mapping.

Mapping, writes McLean, "when viewed as a situated, collective process rather than a representative artefact with inherent meaning, has a creative potential to reveal the unseen, ephemeral and imagined" (2018, p. 76). Her smellmaps use participatory research, in which "smellnotes" are collected by participants to generate maps that "visualize the lived experience of a place" and show "how smell guides us today and in the past to food, mates and safety" (2018, pp. 111-112). McLean's research visually maps smell and highlights how intertwined smells are powerful guides in social urban living. Smell maps can document human behaviour in designed spaces as well as support urban social design in the programming of future streetscapes, shops, plazas, event spaces, and food locations. Victoria Henshaw's book *Urban Smellscapes* (2018) is a comprehensive study describing urban smell and its role in design in detail. She refers to smellwalk experiments which are a type of sensewalk similar to Hildegard Westerkamp's soundwalks from the 1970s. Sensewalks, described by Henshaw provide "useful insights about non-visual aspects of the environment and the way people use their senses to perceive the environment around them" (2014, p. 42).

Our olfactory system is important and needs to be nurtured and not excluded in the design process. Smell is social; it communicates weather, disease, diet, attractiveness, culture, and connects us to place. Smell is always present, guiding us through our lives. Designers use memory and our own lived experiences to develop concepts. As we have learned, smell plays a vital role in constructing our memory and experiences. Should we not then attempt to understand how smell can be a factor in our designs? The following exercises focus on olfactory stimuli and how to document the experience in words, visual representation, oral recording, and smell samples.

4.41
The olfactory experience of grass, Samantha Hart, 2018

Exercise 15: Smell Notes

As all authors note, olfactory stimuli can be quite complex to decipher as there can be multiple scents at once that trigger other senses and memories. In this exercise we will attempt to catalogue and break down different scents and their meanings.

1. Find a space that is easily accessible to you. This can be anything from a park, a commercial street, a market, a church, etc.

2. As you move through your chosen space consider the following questions:
   - Do any of these smells elicit certain emotions or memories?
   - Are the smells pleasant or unpleasant?
   - What kinds of colours, words, or textures would you use to describe the scents?
   - How do the scents make you interact with the space you are in? Do you want to linger or do you want to move on?
   - How intense are the smells?
   - How long do you experience them?

3. How might you begin to visually convey what you have experienced? This exercise does not necessarily need to be hand drawn–it can be done in any way you wish, some examples are with words, an audio recording, a video, mapping, collages or creation of smell samples.

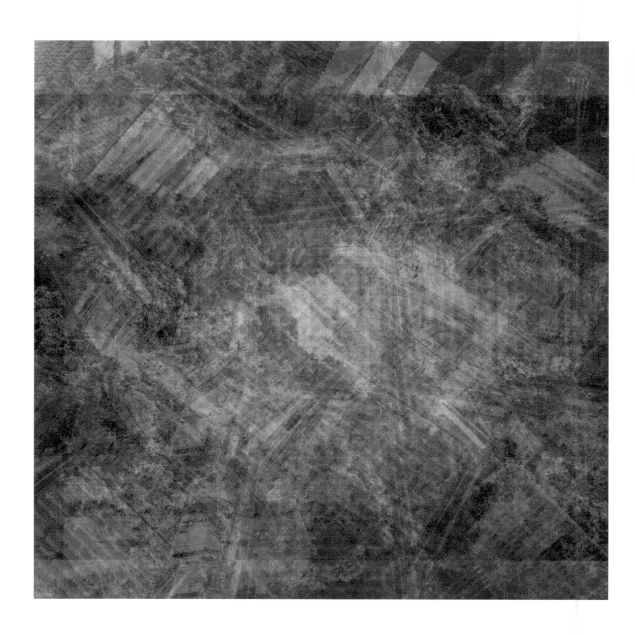

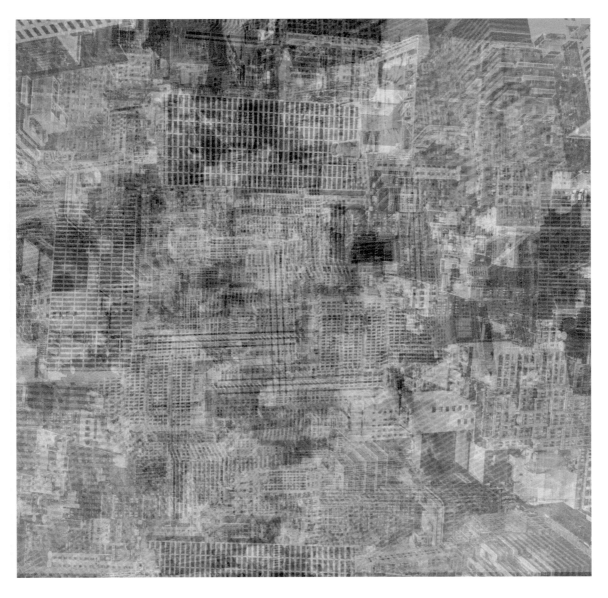

4.42
A comparison of the olfactory experience of New York City (above) and Guangzhou (left), Kemeng Gao, 2018

Exercise 16: Smell Mapping

In this exercise you will create a smell map of any space of your choosing. It could be your urban neighbourhood, an entire city, a village, a park or the natural environment. You will have to come up with a strategy to collect, record, and visualize the olfactory experiences. It is important to do a series of different sessions at different times of the day and different weather conditions as weather heavily impacts smell. Consider also trying this activity for different seasons.

For inspiration read Victoria Henshaw's research on smellwalks and Kate McLean's projects on smellscape mapping.

During your walk consider the following:

- Are there are different smell experiences available?

- How can one categorize smell? Diane Ackerman defines basic categories of smell: "minty (peppermint), floral (roses), ethereal (pears), musky (musk), resinous (camphor), foul (rotten eggs) and acrid (vinegar)" (1990, p. 11). Are there more you could invent?

- What changes the smell experience? Buildings, roads, trees?

- How long do the smells persist? How many smells are there?

- Are there smells that re-occur?

- Are their multiple smells?

- How can a smell's intensity be described and recorded?

4.43 (left)
International smell
map, Mingjia
Chen, 2018

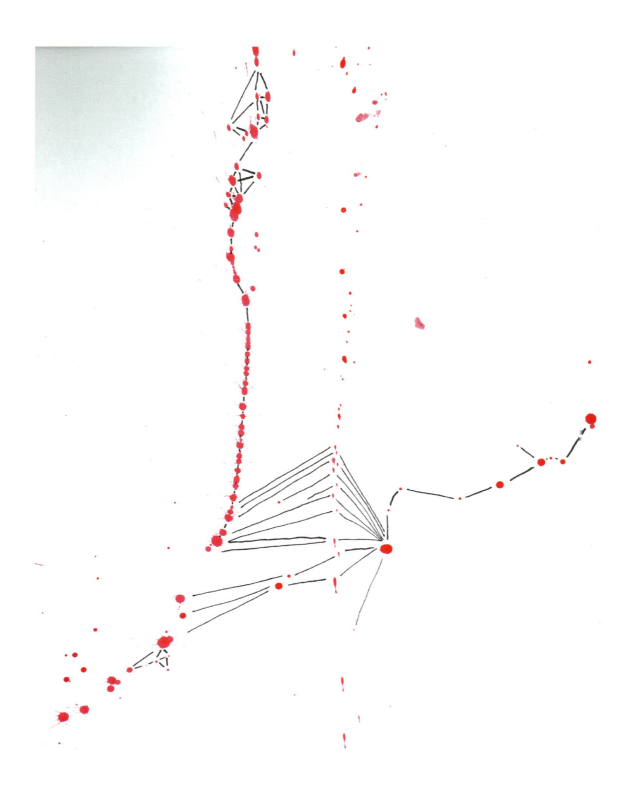

4.44
Smell map of the intersection of Cordova & Cambie, in Vancouver, Canada, Jacob Darowski, 2020

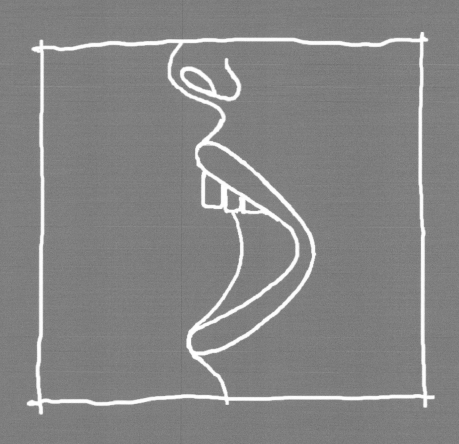

TASTE

Taste is a multisensorial experience. Taste is complex. Tastes change over a person's life; children prefer sweet candy whereas bitter tastes like radicchio or spinach are appreciated by adults. Babies' taste buds are the strongest while after the age of 45 the ability to appreciate taste is reduced. This is generally why older adults add more salt to food and appreciate stronger flavours as "it takes a stronger taste to create the same level of sensation" (Ackerman 1990, pp. 139-140). Like learning to draw, we learn to consciously experience the senses around us, and acquire tastes as we grow (Ackerman 1990, p. 141). The tongue's taste buds, or receptors, can differentiate five different tastes: sweet, salty, sour, bitter, and umami, which the brain catalogues in a "sensory map" that relates to its experiences of distinct flavours (Lupton, 2018a, p. 66).

Taste is not easy to define but its experience is influential in daily living, and that includes design. Industrial designers, interior designers, landscape architects, and architects all deal with taste in their designs—from the inside of buildings, to the streetscape, to farmed and natural environments, and to gardens. Taste impacts how and what we eat, a function that is necessary for survival, like breathing. But while breathing happens unconsciously, the act of eating is a more conscious decision that relies on the individual and the environment around us, which provides the hunting ground to obtain food. All environments are influenced by taste, from how food is hunted and gathered, to how it is transported, delivered, packaged, prepared, and served. And all these stages include design thinking. In Asian and Middle Eastern countries market spaces are an open and inviting dinner table—the smells, flavours, cooking sounds, and visual displays are designed to activate a multisensorial experience.

It is important to note that taste needs smell in order to be fully experienced. Neuroscientist Gordon M. Shepard notes "that smell and taste are so intertwined, we call the combined sense flavour" (as quoted in Lipps, 2018a, p. 97). When we combine smell with taste, we get flavour, which is where things start to get interesting. Flavour is not just how the food tastes on your tongue; it is a combination of smell, texture, and the visual appearance. Taste is like a musical composition using all of the other senses to heighten the tasting experience. Chefs are designers of food; they understand how taste works and how components are layered to create a balanced dish (Kunz and Kaminsky, 2001, p. 4).

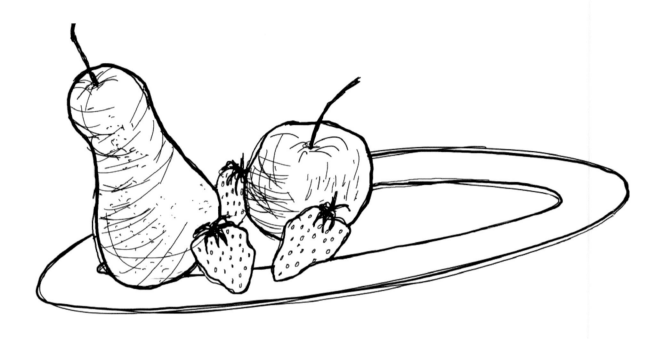

4.45
Plastic food, adapted from *The Senses: Design beyond Vision*, drawn by the author, 2020

Much like a balanced dish, design is a series of components that make a whole. Not only does the sense of smell create flavour, but flavour can also be influenced by the physical appearance of the food. The ripeness of fruit, a bright to dark red colour in strawberries signals freshness while a grey tone suggests that we should not eat it. Colour increases the experience of taste and flavour—the red in jellybeans or cherries communicates a sweet taste (Lipps, 2018a, p. 103). The shape and texture of the food as we consume it also influences its flavour perception, otherwise known as "mouthfeel" (Lipps, 2018a, p. 100). Food engineers study how shapes and visual appearance are associated to a taste—for instance sweetness generally appears to be round and bitterness appears to be angular. (Lipps, 2018a, p. 101). Designers should understand that taste creation is a multi-layered process of many senses acting together. "We eat with our eyes before we even take a bite, translating cues about colour, texture, temperature, and ripeness that change what we taste," summarizes Lipps (2018a, p. 105).

Taste can play a key role in object design. Understanding taste complexity—the visual appearance, colour, smell, and flavour supports designers' intentions to create spaces and objects that can enhance the food experiences. Designers and researchers are developing tools to outthink and outwit eating desires through objects like packaging and tableware (Lipps, 2018a, p. 98). These tools use "visual perception" to give the consumer the illusion that you have more on your table than you actually do in a restaurant context through the placing of physical fake food on your "platescape," a term coined by consumer psychologist Brian Wansink (Lipps, 2018a, p. 98).

Taste also has a perceptional and experiential role to play in the design of buildings and landscapes. John Ruskin once referred to his travels in Verona saying, "I should like to eat this Verona touch by touch" (as quoted in Pallasmaa, 2005, p. 59). The visual perception of the beautiful city of Verona is so strong that Ruskin uses the metaphor touch to express his amazement of the city's architectural beauty and his desire to taste those different experiences literally. Even today we commonly refer to "eating our way through cities." Food is central to how our cities operate; the vibrancy of a city or space often depends on the type and quality of food available. Taste is a vital consideration when designing indoor and outdoor eating spaces. Integrating the sensorial experience of food into the design of spaces—including auditory (sound made by chewing and consuming food), visual perception (colour and placement of food), and touching (feeling of the food while eating, such as dry, greasy, soft, hard, or chewy) will enrich those spaces. Taste is as important as the air we breathe, and a designer's awareness of this sense can be practiced with the following exercises.

4.46
"I was inspired by the partnership of the salty and sweet, which work together to frame the experience. Their rhythm is interrupted by the other flavours but ultimately they work together to create a singular whole," Kathryn Pierre, 2020

Exercise 17: Taste Rave

This exercise attempts to experience taste—an extremely complex task. As you explore a public market or a grocery store, try to describe (smell, taste, feel, hear, and see) the different kinds of food that you are tasting. Purchase or try three different items, preferably something that you have never tried before. Close your eyes and begin to think about the different tastes and your body's reaction to them.

Some prompts as you taste test:

- How does the food make you feel?

- Does the taste remind you of other food, memories, spaces?

- Do you like the taste? Do you dislike the taste?

- What kinds of colours, words, or textures would you use to describe the taste?

- Does the food make a sound when you eat it?

- What is its temperature and texture?

- How does it smell?

Intensity

Peeling sound like
opening velcro

Intensity

Intensity

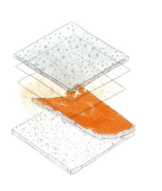

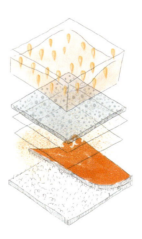

Spongey sound of
separating orange
segments

Biting through film
to experience cold
juicy sensation

197

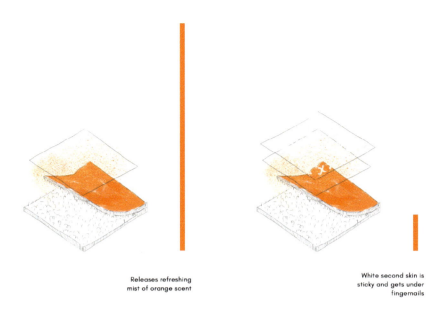
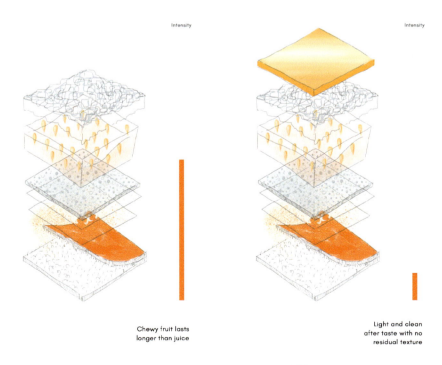

4.47
The experience of eating an orange,
Marissa Campbell, 2020

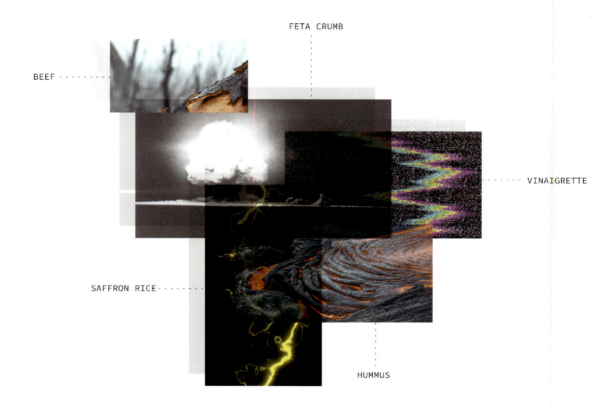

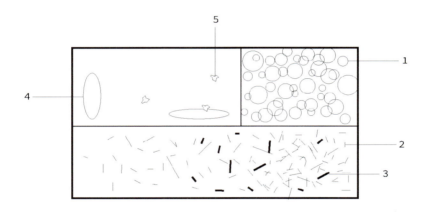

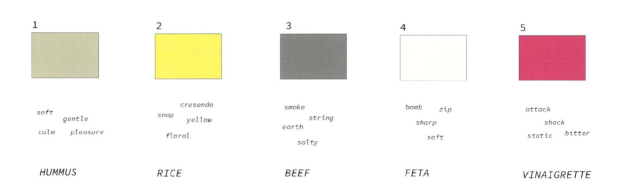

1	2	3	4	5
soft gentle calm pleasure	cresendo snap yellow floral	smoke string earth salty	bomb zip sharp soft	attack shock static bitter
HUMMUS	RICE	BEEF	FETA	VINAIGRETTE

4.48
Analysis of a beef shawarma platter, Berend Kessler, 2020

4.49
Vessel sketches,
Jacob Darowski,
2020

Exercise 18: Design a Drinking Object

This exercise was inspired by reading the chapter in *The Senses-Design beyond Vision* on "Flavour" (pp. 66-71) by Ellen Lupton and "The Sensory Table" (pp. 94-107) by Andrea Lipps. Lipps describes in her chapter how fake food, applied to fill the plate, reduces eating habits. The artist Marije Vogelzang pioneered work in eating design, creating food "prosthetics" that appear like real food, filling the plate so less food is eaten (Lipps, 2018a, p. 99).

This exercise takes this idea in another direction and asks for a drinking tool to be designed which gives the perception of drinking a full glass of alcohol or soft drink while actually drinking much less. Could the same idea be used to create a glass conveying the perception of being full but in actual fact it is not?

Starting out one should ask questions such as:

- How does the liquid move?
- What is the colour and texture of the liquid?
- What is the form and how can there appear to be more liquid?
- How can the liquid be covered up or simulated?
- How is the alcohol or sweet smell controlled and reduced?
- What material is it made of?
- How heavy is it?
- What is the colour?

Draw out these ideas; try to model them physically or using 3D software.

Recoommended Reads

On Drawing
Drawing on the Right Side of the Brain, Betty Edwards (1979)
This book is a pedagogically thorough resource to learn how to draw. In its fourth edition, it is a seasoned book to help the reader learn to draw. It also explains the relationship between drawing skill and cognitive action using many examples, and it highlights the importance of drawing in the design process. .

Drawn to Design: Analyzing Architecture through Freehand Drawing, Eric J. Jenkins (2013)
This book is a guide for analytical sketching in architecture. It explains the drawing process as a means of design exploration providing the techniques necessary to develop concepts. It clarifies the value of free hand drawing as a fundamental design skill in education and practice.

Lines: A Brief History, Tim Ingold (2007)
Tim Ingold spent a large amount of his career researching and writing about lines. This book is a philosophical discourse on lines—examining how the line takes form in the nature, place, and the printed world.

@Linescapes, Instagram
This Instagram platform run by landscape architects Sonja Rozman Habjanic and Gaspar Habjanic from Berlin provides short thorough tutorials on freehand landscape and architectural sketching. The site is updated daily and they provide daily question and answer sessions.

@Futurelandscapes, Instagram
This Instagram platform is run by designer and landscape architect Stephanie Braconnier and provides longer tutorial sessions on how to create digital landscape architectural renderings. The tutorials also engage the learner in the larger landscape context of a project thereby learning to observe the complexity of the environment.

On Referential Sketching
Architecture: Form, Space and Order, Francis D. K. Ching (2015)
Francis Ching's many drawing books teach all the foundations of architectural drawing and are a useful resource to begin to understand how one might go about drawing space, particularly built space.

Drawing for Landscape Architecture: Sketch to Screen to Site, Edward Hutchinson (2016)
Edward Hutchinson's book serves as a resource for inspiration about how one might begin to analyze landscapes. He places a particular emphasis on the importance of hand drawing, but also shows how this can be then taken to the computer.

Drawing for Landscape Architects, Sabrina Wilk, (2015)
This book is a valuable resource for those looking to better understand how to draw landscape architectural elements from all scales and views. It is comprehensive in its graphics and it is recommended to try tracing over the graphics in this book to grasp landscape architectural graphic conventions.

On Analytical Sketching
Form and Fabric in Landscape Architecture: A Visual Introduction, Catherine Dee (2001)
Catherine Dee is an artist and landscape architect who explains complex landscape processes and systems at different scales. She uses hand drawing as a tool to develop diagrams, annotated sketches, and mapping of different landscape processes.

Eames Office, Powers of 10 (1977)
This film available online teaches the importance and understanding of scale from the universe to a carbon atom. Charles and Ray Eames' short film is one of the most influential films ever made on scale and is considered a foundational video for new designers to watch.

Visual Notes for Architects and Designers, Norman Crowe and Paul Laseau (1984)
This fundamental book on visual literacy provides examples of visual note-taking and theoretical background knowledge needed to see the world through drawing.

Designers with Sketching Examples
David Adjaye
Alvar Alto
Tadao Ando
Francis D.K. Ching
Le Corbusier
Chris T. Cornelius
Cathrine Dee
Es Devlin
Garret Eckbo
Olafur Eliasson
Norman Foster
Konstantin Gricic
Michael Graves
Zaha Hadid
Lawrence Halprin
Frank Lloyd Wright
Erich Mendelsohn
Frits Palmboom
Renzo Piano
Ronald Rael
Dieter Rams
Richard Rogers
Hans Scharoun
Janet Swailes
Michael Van Valkenburgh

On Photography

The Eye is the Door: Photography and the Art of Visual Thinking, Anne Whiston Spirn (2014)
This book describes photography as not only a seeing and recording tool but also a visual thinking tool to expose design problems at all scales visually to provide solutions. We highly recommend the book for designers looking to use photography as an essential part of their analysis and observation process.

On Photography, Susan Sontag (1973)
This fundamental book on photography is a compilation of essays expressing the history of photography and provides Susan Sontag's personal view on photography in the politically changing times of the 1970s.

A Short Story of Photography, Walter Benjamin (1931)
This essay explores the consequences photography would have globally at a period of time where there was drastic technological and political change. It provides insight on how photography's influence increased through the improved reproduction technology in the first half of the 20th century, and how this increased reproduction made photos a common commodity instead of an individual's artistic expression.

Ways of Seeing, John Berger (1972)
This fundamental book describes how we see and understand pictures through an art historical lens. It provides different methods for how to view pictures and suggests methods of how to see, learn, and interpret art in multiple ways.

On Hearing

Soundscape and the Built Environment, Jiang Kang and Brigitte Schulte-Fortkamp ed. (2016)
This book systematically discusses current soundscapes in the built environment. It provides theory and basic background, and explains what a soundscape is, how is it important, and how does it affect people in terms of their health and perception of the acoustic environment. The book also explains tools for implementing a soundscape approach, with measurement techniques, mapping, and good soundscape practices, and describes examples of the application of the soundscape approach in planning, design, and assessment.

Wednesday is Indigo Blue: Discovering the Brain of Synesthesia, Richard Cytowic and David Eagleman (2011)
This book explains the current research that exists on synesthesia—how our brains do this and what it looks like. It's an interesting read to see how and why our brains make certain associations.

Kids Describe Color to a Blind Person, The Cut, (2017)
Available on YouTube, children are asked to try and describe colours to someone who cannot see colours. The responses are quite funny and prompt thinking about how to describe something that is so visual.

"Soundwalking" Autumn Leaves, Sound and the Environment in Artistic Practice, Hildegard Westerkamp (2007)
This article is easily available online and we highly recommend that you read it to learn

more about soundscapes. It details and guides you along solitary and group soundwalks and introduces different sound descriptions to learn the difference between "hearing and listening" (Westerkamp, 2007, pp. 49-58). Her instructions begin with having students first choose an outdoor space. She then prescribes a series of activities to heighten your listening skills. Students are recommended to walk around the space and begin to note different aspects of the space—for instance if the walk is more pleasing acoustically or visually. She describes how to have a dialogue with different sounds you may come across; for instance, copying a bird singing and observing—"listening" to—its reaction and response.

On Smelling
"Scentscape" in The Senses: Design beyond Vision, Andrea Lipps (2018)
Lipps provides an updated version on olfactory research and design and includes innovative research into olfactory visualization/mapping, building materials in architecture, interior design, and cosmetics.

Urban Smellscapes, Victoria Henshaw (2014)
This book comprehensively examines smell theory and design practice of scholars, artists, and professionals who are interested in smell and how to design smell-inclusive places/spaces in cities. It is the first of its kind in examining the role of smell specifically in contemporary experiences and perceptions of English towns and cities, highlighting the perception of urban smellscapes as inter-related with place perception, and describing smell's contribution towards overall sense of place. With case studies from factories, breweries, urban parks, and experimental smell environments, the book identifies processes by which urban smell environments are managed and controlled, and gives designers and city managers tools to actively use smell in their work. The book provides a deep scholastic and urban design focused book in which she summarizes current knowledge and her own research on smells and how to design with smell in the urban environment. The whole book is a comprehensive contemporary insight into smell in urban design.

Designing with Smell, Victoria Henshaw (2018)
This book aims to inspire designers to actively consider smell in their work. It provides practical guidance regarding different equipment, techniques, stages, and challenges which might be encountered as part of this process. Throughout the text there is an emphasis on spatial design in numerous forms and interpretations in the urban environment, as well as the representation of spatial relationships with smell.

On Tasting
The Elements of Taste, Gray Kunz and Peter Kaminsky (2001)
This book describes how chefs define taste and its complex, intertwined relationships with the other senses. The introduction is of particular interest as it attempts to categorize and describe a myriad of tastes in a way that is poetic and visual.

"Flavour" in The Senses: Design beyond Vision, Ellen Lupton (2018)
This chapter describes how smell and taste are intertwined physically with each other in the human body. The taste buds and olfactory/smell receptors work hand in hand to create flavour. The chapter also describes how flavour impacts visual and tactile perception and how the brain fuses them.

References

Ackerman, D. (1990). *A Natural History of the Senses*. New York, NY: Random House.

Adams, M., Bruce, N., Davies, W. J., Cain, R., Jennings, P., Carlyle, A., Cusack, P., Hume, K., & Plack, C. (2007). Soundwalking as a methodology for understanding soundscapes. *Proceedings of the Institute of Acoustics, 30*(2), 1-7.

Ambroziak B. M. (2005). *Michael Graves: Images of a Grand Tour*. Princeton: Princeton Architectural Press.

Benjamin, W. (1931/1972). A Short History on Photography. *Screen, 13*(1), 5-26. https://doi.org/10.1093/screen/13.1.5

Bourbonne, A. (2018). Tactile Sound. In E. Lupton & A. Lipps (Eds.), *The Senses: Design beyond Vision*, (pp. 148-155). New York, NY: Princeton Architecture Press.

Cerwéna, G., Kreutzfeldt, J., & Wingren, C. (2017). "Soundscape actions: A tool for noise treatment based on three workshops in landscape architecture." *Frontiers of Architectural Research, 6*(4), 505-518. https://doi.org/10.1016/j.foar.2017.10.002

Copeland, L. (2017, Jan. 5). *Feel the Music—Literally—With Some Help from New Synesthesia Research*. Smithsonian. Retrieved from https://bit.ly/2lY0F6o

Crowe, N. & Laseau, P. (2012). *Visual Notes for Architects and Designers*. Hoboken, NJ: John Wiley & Sons.

Dee, C. (2001). *Form and Fabric in Landscape Architecture: A Visual Introduction*. New York, NY: Routledge.

Eiliat, H., & Pusca, D. (2013). Teaching and learning experience using digital sketching. *2013 3rd Interdisciplinary Engineering Design Education Conference*, pp. 134-138. doi: 10.1109/IEDEC.2013.6526774

Have, R., & van der Toorn, M. (2012). The role of hand drawing in basic design education in the digital age. *International Conference on Engineering and Mathematics*, Bangalore, 2012, pp. 72-80. Les Ulis: EDP Sciences.

Henshaw, V. (2014). *Urban Smellscapes: Understanding and Designing City Smell Environments*. New York, NY: Routledge.

Hutchinson Guest, A. (1990). Dance Notation. *Perspecta, 26*, 203-214.

Jenkins, E. J. (2013). *Drawn to Design*. Basel, CH: Birkhauser.

Kunz, G. & Kaminsky, P. (2001). Introduction. In *The Elements of Taste*, (2-21). New York, NY: Little, Brown and Company,

Landau, S. (2018). Drawing by Touching. In E. Lupton & A. Lipps (Eds.), *The Senses: Design beyond Vision*, (pp. 176-177). New York, NY: Princeton Architecture Press.

Leatherbarrow, D. (1998). Showing what otherwise hides itself. *Harvard Design Magazine*, 50-55.

Lipps, A. (2018a). Scentscape. In E. Lupton & A. Lipps (Eds.), *The Senses: Design beyond Vision*, (108 -121). New York, NY: Princeton Architecture Press

Lipps, A. (2018b). The Sensory Table. In E. Lupton & A. Lipps (Eds.), *The Senses: Design beyond Vision*, (pp. 94-107). New York, NY: Princeton Architecture Press.

Lupton, E. (2018a). Notes on Touch, Sound, Smell, and Flavor. In E. Lupton & A. Lipps (Eds.), *The Senses: Design beyond Vision*, (pp. 36-66). New York, NY: Princeton Architecture Press.

Lupton, E. (2018b). Tactile Graphics. In E. Lupton & A. Lipps (Eds.), *The Senses: Design beyond Vision*, (pp. 158-175). New York, NY: Princeton Architecture Press.

Lupton, E. (2018c). Visualizing Sound. In E. Lupton & A. Lipps (Eds.), *The Senses: Design beyond Vision*, (pp. 204-217). New York, NY: Princeton Architecture Press.

Mau, B. (2018). Designing LIVE: A new medium for the senses. In E. Lupton & A. Lipps (Eds.), *The Senses: Design beyond Vision*, (pp. 20-23). New York, NY: Princeton Architecture Press.

McLean, K. (2018). Communicating and mediating smeelscapes: The design and exposition of olfactory mappings. In V. Henshaw, K. McLean, D. Medway, C. Perkins & G. Warnaby (Eds.), *Designing with Smell: Practices, Techniques and Challenges*, (pp. 67-77). New York, NY: Routledge.

Mooney, P. (2019). *Planting Design, Connecting People and Place*. New York, NY: Routledge.

Pallasmaa, J. (2005). *The Eyes of the Skin*. West Sussex, UK: Wiley Publishing.

Sacks, O. (2007). *Musicophilia*. New York, NY: Alfred A. Knopf, Inc.

Sontag, S. (1973). *On Photography*. New York: Farrar, Straus and Giroux.

Tufte, E. W. (1990). *Envisioning Information*. Cheshire, CT: Graphics Press.

Unwin, S. (2007). Analyzing architecture through drawing. *Building Research & Information*, 35(1), 101–110. doi: 10.1080/09613210600879881

Westerkamp, H. (2007). Soundwalking. In A. Carlyle (Ed.), *Autumn Leaves, Sound and the Environment in Artistic Practice*, (pp. 49-58). Paris: Double Entendre

Whiston Spirn, A. (2014). *The Eye Is a Door: Landscape, Photography, and the Art of Discovery*. Boston, MA: Wolf Tree Press.

Chapter 5

Teaching Multisensorial Literacy

5.1
Potsdamer Platz Hotel
Green Roof, drawn by
the author, 1996

Teaching Multi-Sensory Design

While historically sight has been the emphasized sense in design teaching, there needs to be a shift in pedagogy to include all the senses. However, re-learning to see not simply with our eyes but with our entire bodies is not just a task for students. Instructors also need to integrate the five senses more actively in their design studios, lecture courses, and seminars. This chapter provides suggestions for instructors to teach beyond visual literacy and consider instead teaching multisensorial literacy. These suggestions are based mostly on the author's own professional and academic experience training landscape architecture and architecture students for more than 20 years in Europe and North America.

As multisensorial literacy is part of foundational design education, it should be taught from the beginning to the end of spatial design degrees with a strong emphasis during the first year. The first year of design school is one of the most influential and impactful in design education and it is here that foundational design skills are developed. It is therefore recommended that the most experienced and seasoned design teachers are engaged for this task—more experienced professors should be teaching first-year students. Extensive design teaching knowledge and pedagogical experience are needed to convey the complex design process visually, orally, and as the author additionally recommends, multisensorially. In North American design schools, for example, less experienced instructors typically teach first-year students because the more senior instructors would like, or are encouraged by their universities, to focus more on research. They also often see teaching the first-year as being more labour intensive and time consuming during the semester. While it can be at times demanding to teach earlier years, it can also be very rewarding helping students strive to become designers. It is paramount that design education begins with solid foundational design knowledge and a skill set of design thinking from site immersion to ideation. Teaching students again in the upper years will be more rewarding if they are able to develop a rigorous foundation in their first year. This will in turn reduce the teaching load in the upper years to enable professors to focus more on research and creativity.

Multisensorial literacy however is not only important in the design profession. Medical students learn anatomy by drawing, as do botany students in order to understand the details of a plant, and engineers for the complexity of machines.). Multisensorial diagnostics were once important in the medical profession, however the advancement in radiology has initiated a decrease in doctors' abilities to smell a disease, or touch and listen to the sound of symptoms (Whiston Spirn, 2014, p. 115). Training students to rely on their senses as important recording devices is on the decline. Whiston Spirn argues that we should continue to teach multisensorial literacy, even outside of the design world. For instance, medical students looking at art can study skin colour, posture, and learn to distinguish between different patterns of form to develop an understanding of patients and their condition (Whiston Spirn, 2014, p. 116).

Drawing is a readily available learning tool that can bring awareness to the sense of sight and with it an interest in including the other senses in the multisensorial design process. Practicing drawing increases the skill of visual thinking (Whiston Spirn, 2014, p 115). Training students to communicate through hand-drawing is on the decline. Studying art, especially the works of the masters, can help everyone learn to see. Drawing, observing, and learning about art stimulates the mind to better understand colour, texture, composition, and complexity.

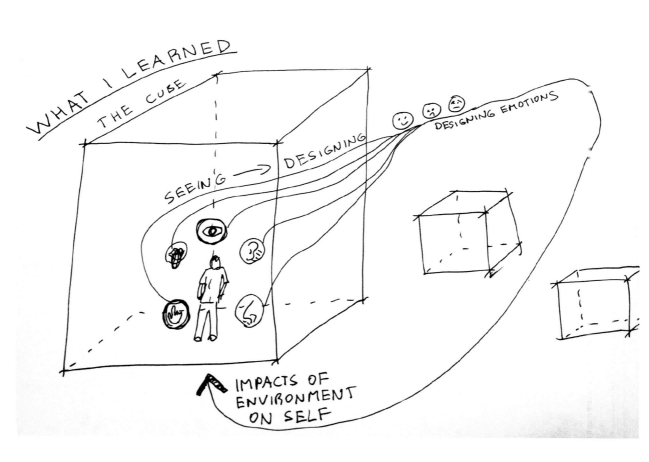

5.2
Class summary,
Jonathan Behnke, 2020

David Drazil, notes that there has been a resurgence of analog drawing skills in design. As students are encouraged to learn how to utilize digital software above all else, the emphasis on hand drawing is often sidelined. He notes that there is more demand for analog drawing skills now, in particular for design communication and idea development as digital software often cannot fulfill this need (Flores, 2019). The creative design process is often missing in digital drawing, whereas "sketching is the instant connection of head and mind" (Flores, 2019).

Multisensorial literacy is the key to critical and creative thinking. It helps students to deeply understand for example, the difference between accessible and inclusive design. While a ramp provides access for wheelchairs in a museum, it does not provide inclusive access for all visitors. For instance, if the visitor is visually impaired, they will interact with the museum and its exhibits very differently from someone who has 20/20 vision. Instructors, therefore, need to be mindful of how they teach the design process for inclusivity. It starts by addressing inclusive design at all design process stages, as laid out in Chapter 2 of this book, beginning with the site immersion stage, and ending with design ideas. In the design process, instructors should reiterate including all design users in their design process. Acquiring multisensorial literacy permits students to consider more deeply how the senses are used in the environment and how they provide a knowledge base that informs design learning.

Skill Training

Skill can be regarded as trained practice (Swailes, 2016, p. 46). Learning a new skill is much like learning a new language and can only truly be successful through practice and repetition. The same could be said about learning to sketch or draw. Landscape architect Janet Swailes writes "practice remains interesting through its structure using the hand and eye, with people learning and improving through repetition...repetition through tracing provides practice in terms of both drawing skills and a deeper engagement and familiarity with the subject" (2016, p. 46). If the pedagogical processes of how we teach sketching and drawing through practice are considered, one could use this method to teach multisensorial perception. The author suggests that the method of learning by repetition could be extended to practice interpreting all senses. The corporal recording mechanisms of the ear and skin, hands and feet, and mouth and nose should be trained in design education to be consciously activated to practice multisensorial literacy. The author suggests that repeating multisensorial perception exercises in design education, is as important as a skill for students as drawing and field sketching.

There is a call in design schools to place more emphasis on learning as a process—that mistakes, and at times failures, are inevitable and okay. There is beauty in practice and improvement, and as educators, we owe it to our students to teach them the importance of recognizing and valuing the process as much as or even more than the final outcome. Practice is a vital part of the skill-building process, and this needs to be encouraged. Another aspect is teaching students to "let go." As Swailes notes on her experiences with teaching students field sketching, learning to let go is recognized in the practice of skills competency, and "repetition...corrects imperfections" (2016, p. 46).

Further, the pressure to teach digital tools has extensively reduced our tendency to encourage communication through hand sketching. This is a dilemma, as sketching is a visual thinking process and allows for a quick visual record by the students to be effectively

5.3
"Interpreting and representing the unique, multisensorial experiences we each have is a crucial and under-valued communication skill. Our perception of objects, spaces, and senses varies, and designer must consider the range in sensation that they are introducing to their audiences," Mariah Campbell, 2020

reviewed and critiqued by an instructor. It is suggested that design instructors today should still practice and encourage hand drawing as a part of the design process—and to hand draw themselves as they instruct on an individual basis or in front of the entire class. We also recommend that at a minimum, students keep sketchbooks, and professors place an academic importance on hand sketching and annotation. This could primarily be achieved through regular checks on students' work along with positive regular reinforcement and critique of the design process. There could also be an emphasis on grading the effort in process and thinking rather than the final outcome.

Syllabus Design

For teaching the senses, a structured syllabus with clear goals is important. Reading should be encouraged but not forced. To make sure that reading for each session is carried out by the students, the selection of the topics and length of the readings should focus on the observation of each sense alone first before they are synthesized in the analysis and design process. This will keep students focused on one topic and allow them to become familiar with the individual senses. Roughly 15-30 pages a week is suggested for first-year undergraduate students. There should be a balance between scholarly rigour of theoretical understanding and the transfer of that knowledge through practicing observation of the senses and recording them in the environment.

It is suggested that the readings are discussed at the beginning of each seminar, lecture course, and in studios. The assignments on visual and multisensorial literacy could, for example, be integrated with 3- to 5-hour exercises in the studio, lecture course or seminar, or a whole course or seminar could be taught on the senses. The author currently teaches such a course at the University of British Columbia.

It is also important to make sure the syllabus is not too prescriptive in wording and deliverables. The syllabus should encourage thinking by doing. For example: encourage observation through site immersion, field recording, analysis, and design synthesis with the sensorial observation exercises described in Chapter 4. An open-ended assignment with a series of prompts will challenge the students to record and describe beyond the visual and choose their own recording method they feel comfortable with, for example, with sound or video recording and a transcription into text and drawings. Some exercises should have opportunities for comparing sensorial perception among students, to encourage the discussion of the individual sensorial observations. For example, students tasting or smelling the same food and can compare their experience, by describing the taste or smell visually, orally, as text, sound recording, or with video or podcasts, or as a combination of different recordings. It is important for the instructor to balance artistic non-prescribed exercises with prescribed comparison exercises. The idea of artistic non-prescribed exercises is to broaden the student's creative thinking strategies for how to observe and record the senses, instead of teaching them a more prescribed set of smells or tastes.

The assignment deliverables should be open ended at first, as any deliverable restrictions tend to hinder creativity in presentation. If documentation is required, the students should learn to figure it out for themselves. Often documentation is very prescriptive to satisfy the instructor's need to document their own teaching work for tenure and promotion, instead of thinking of the student's presentation skill learning needs. This defeats the important purpose of experimentation in pedagogy—for students to learn and discover oral presentation and layout techniques by doing it completely themselves.

Online Teaching

With the COVID 19 epidemic, teaching has changed dramatically and perhaps forever. Teaching multisensorial literacy online is not at a disadvantage compared to traditional onsite teaching; it is just a different format of teaching. It opens up global opportunities for seeing the environment and encourages students to engage with their direct communities and environments. The class time is spent focusing on on-screen learning to observe and record while the instructor uses a tablet to visualize their teaching content. It is paramount that the instructor writes a script or storyboard beforehand, with the main components of the lecture visualized in images and annotated. This will visually frame and focus the lecture content but leaves it open for additional content to be added during online class time. As everything is recorded, one must see this lecture time as an interactive teaching performance. It is paramount for students to have an asynchronous lecture and teaching experience. Short breaks should be provided after 30-40 minute sessions. There should be space for students to communicate with each other and connect inside and outside of the classroom. Create short online exercises during class which can be carried out by the students in their direct environment to initiate the seeing, recording, and analyzing process through drawing. The exercises should be short (15-30 minutes), and easily adaptable to their environments. For example, an exercise could entail recording the flow of rain on their building. The whole session should be recorded for students to access later to review and reiterate what they have learned. Further, the students' work can be screen shared in class, discussed, and reviewed by the peers and instructor. A recorded lecture also allows the instructor to review their performance, giving them more precise advice on how to improve.

This method practices observation and drawing with immediate feedback. During the week, the students can review the recording and then complete their own assignments locally. The completed assignments can then be uploaded on an online platform for the instructor and peers to review. Online teaching widens the environmental field of vision to observe from local to global sites, creating an internationally inclusive design education. It allows students to learn about each other's personal culture and environments as the assignments can be carried out anywhere. Research has shown that screen time is more valuable and effective as a learning tool, as long it is interactive, with small assignments carried out online, conversation initiated and with it thinking stimulated. A pre-recorded video or movie without active participation will take away that cognitive creative process of recording the observations. Watching a pre-recorded movie or video is passive; the director and actors have created the images, and it only stimulates sight and sound. The other senses taste, touch, and smell are excluded. Online live recorded teaching, however, is adaptive and interactive, and therefore is a teaching tool. Observing the environment is a cognitive process where "mental imagery" is practiced through the multi-sensory experience on site (Suggate & Martzog, 2020, p. 3).

Fear of Failure

It takes many years of practice until drawing becomes an unconscious skill to be used as a thinking tool, like being a skilled driver or professional musician, just as it takes many years of practice until a piano player can improvise a melody. Sketching is not taught often enough in design education, and when it is taught, it is mostly in brief, introductory courses.

There is not enough emphasis on sketching throughout the entire design education process, as the focus tends to be on mastering digital drawing tools.

There are multiple ways in which fear of failure can be experienced by students. For instance, researchers have found that the primary emotion that derives from fear of failure is shame. Students may avoid uncertain or unfavourable tasks or events to avoid the feeling of shame. Students can develop a learned helplessness so that they are conditioned to accept failure (Choi, 2020, pp. 3-4). Here, we may see instances where a student will describe themselves as a "bad drawer" to avoid the shame of failing. We know that failure and mistakes are necessary for improvement. In my experiences, one of the biggest challenges in teaching students to sketch is addressing their fear that the images they have drawn do not adequately explain the content they are recording, as well as their concern with how the sketch is drawn in terms of its accuracy and line expression. This causes students to freeze and either not draw at all or compare their skillset with other students. The inexperienced sketcher is often left thinking too much about how to draw rather than using sketching as a tool to think (Jenkins, 2013, p. 30).

How might we create this kind of open environment? Instructors should consider how they might want to teach students how to think through sketching. It is here where the instructor has an opportunity to support students in overcoming their fear. If assignments are focused too much on drawing accurately and precisely, rather than providing a space to play and experiment, then the students might find it difficult to express themselves. It is the instructor's responsibility to choose exercises that incite engaged thinking and playful recording, creating a space where sketching can become an important tool when thinking about space. We have had good outcomes with teaching through animated visualizations done by the instructor prior to class. The exercises should encourage students to record in their own style, rather than attempting to record precisely what they see in front of them. Seeing is also hearing, smelling, tasting, and touching. Encouraging them to engage with their environments multisensorially, for instance by asking them to draw blind fold, will distract them from just being focused on drawing referentially. In a class setting, students who are not experienced drawers often freeze when they see other students drawing more confidently. This fear accelerates when students are put on the spot in front of more experienced sketchers. Thus, any form of review that examines their work more in depth should focus on content rather than accuracy.

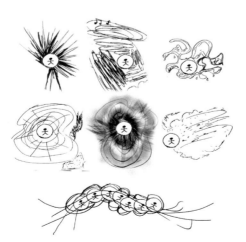

5.4
Class Summary,
Doug Craig, 2020

5.5
Drawing class at the Museum of Anthropology, in Vancouver, Canada, 2015

How do professionals teach students to be free of this fear? Architect David Drazil suggests that we need to encourage failure as an essential component to becoming a strong designer; "to fail as often and as early as possible...the more you fail during the process, the better the result at the end" (Flores, 2019). A good way to avoid fear of failure in students, is by beginning the course with basic drawing skills but also ensuring that the assignments given introduce playful elements to these skill-building exercises, for instance, practicing drawing straight lines, but also exploring how simple lines can convey emotions or actions. Giving the students joy with achievable, motivating exercises is important. Drawing is, after all, a physical and cognitive skill (Jenkins, 2013, p. 31). It is important to provide readings and theory drawing from skilled sketchers and scholars to provide an intellectual background around why and how to practice drawing. Working with narratives and metaphors, such as the explanation of practicing piano to become a confident musician or training to become a professional athlete, can reinforce in a student's mind that drawing is a skill that can be practiced and thereby learned.

Playfulness and experimentation are key in teaching this content. While we want students to learn important technical skills, we also want to encourage creativity. A study done with students in the Faculty of Architecture at Kraków University of Technology (Kraków, Poland) found that when creative drawing and painting was incorporated into the students' study program, there was a positive effect on the rest of their curriculum. The study found that the students developed a greater imagination and creative awareness and that the art of drawing and painting supplemented the technical foundations of the curriculum (Domarzewski, 2019).

Instagram and YouTube have become online platforms for the sketching community, new and old, to learn about sketching and overcoming the fear of putting pen to paper. Tired of the rigidity that can arise with digital drawing tools, many young designers have begun examining their relationships with freehand sketching. Two platforms are especially of interest: "Sketch like an Architect" by David Drazil, and "Linescapes" by Rozman Habjanic and Gasper Habjanic. Habjanic and Habjanic had a professor in school who not only taught them to sketch, but also instilled in them a passion and knowledge to teach others. All three designers see Instagram as a valuable medium for teaching hand drawing skills, providing daily drawing tutorials and methods to encourage the ideation process.

Site Visits

In first year in particular, and regularly throughout the first professional design degrees, project sites for studio courses should be chosen locally and be easily accessible to allow for students to immerse themselves in the site.

To teach visual and multisensorial literacy, regular site visits with the instructor are important, rather than only visiting the site at the beginning of a project. It is suggested that instructors visit a site at least three times at the stages of (1) observation (site immersion) and recording process, (2) analysis process, and (3) ideation process. This will allow for the students to engage repeatedly with the environmental context in which they are designing. It will support their understanding of how to perceive, read, and analyze a design problem in its surrounding context with all senses. Observation, recording, analysis, and synthesis of ideas are all part of design, and teaching should encourage going back and forth between the three.

Multi-Sensorial Teaching Check List

Preparation Stage	Suggested Directions
1. Instructor selection	Balance seasoned and unseasoned instructors in first year
2. Prepare course content about the senses	For seminars and courses prepare 2-3 papers to read per week For studio 2 papers to read per week Consider other types of multimedia that may be more relevant than readings
3. Prepare syllabus	For seminars and courses weekly assignments For studio projects integrate assignments throughout the overarching design assignment
4. Prepare assignments	In seminars and courses balance prescribed and nonprescribed tasks and encourage comparative observations and studies For studio integrate the senses throughout the design assignment
5. Prepare regular site visits	For seminars and courses visit weekly For studio a minimum of three times at the observation, analysis and synthesis stage, emphasize that all three stages are "design" and that it is a constant back and forth between all three

Preparation Stage	Suggested Directions
6. Plan regular discussions of readings and observations in class	For seminar and course 1 hour per week For studio integrate discussion throughout the design assignment
7. Initiate assignment upload on blog designed by students	For seminar and courses check in on student performance by instructor weekly For studio a minimum of three times at the observation, analysis and synthesis stage
8. Initiate student lead final presentation	Students show a selection of assignments via projector with video, sound or podcast recordings, or printed, handmade images, collages or models
9. Provide feedback	For seminar and courses during final presentation by reviewers and instructor For studio during presentations and individual student meetings

5.6
Class Summary,
Jacob Darowski, 2020

References

Choi, B. (2020). I'm afraid of not succeeding in learning: Introducing an instrument to measure higher education students' fear of failure in learning. *Studies in Higher Education*, 1-13. doi: 10.1080/03075079.2020.1712691

Domarzewski, A. (2019). Architecture students gain experience from open-air workshops in drawing and painting. *World Transactions on Engineering and Technology Education*, 17(3), 373-378.

Flores, M [host]. (2019, July 23). How can sketching make us better designers? A conversation with David Drazil [audioa podcast episode]. In *The Archiologist*. Retrieved from https://www.sketchlikeanarchitect.com/blog/podcast-advice-to-fresh-graduates-how-to-overcome-fear-of-failure-my-backstory-and-more

Jenkins, E. J. (2013). *Drawn to Design*. Basel: Birkhauser.

Whiston Spirn, A. (2014). *The Eye Is a Door: Landscape, Photography, and the Art of Discovery*. Boston: Wolf Tree Press.

Suggate, S.P. & Martzog, P. (2020). Screen-time influences children's mental imagery performance. *Developmental Science, 23*(6), 1-13. https://doi.org/10.1111/desc.12978

Swailes, J. (2016). *Field Sketching and the Experience of Landscape*. Abingdon: Routledge.

Chapter 6

For an Inclusive Future

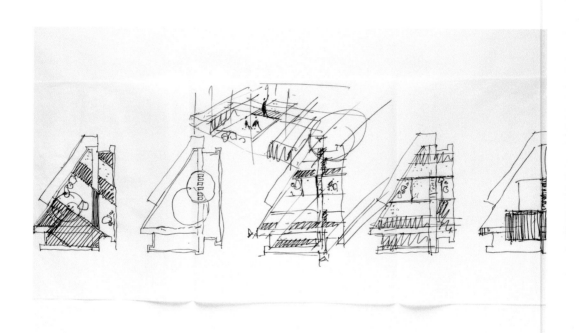

6.1
Thinking through drawing, Potsdamer Platz courtyard design, drawn by the author, 1996

Conclusion

Teaching visual literacy has a long documented theoretical and practiced tradition in design schools. With books by Berger on seeing, Crowe and Laseau on visual notes, Ching on architectural drawing, Jenkins with *Drawn to Design*, Hanks and Bellison with "rapid viz", McKim on experiences in visual thinking, Swailes on field sketching, Sullivan on drawing the landscape, Dee in *Form and Fabric in Landscape Architecture*, Hutchison on drawing for landscape architecture, Whiston Spirn in *The Eye is the Door*, Pallasmaa in *The Eyes of the Skin* and *The Thinking Hand*, Sontag's *On Photography*, Laseau on freehand sketching, and Treib on *Drawing/Thinking* to name a few, the wealth of knowledge on suggested theories and practices about visual literacy over the last 40 years by so many scholars has helped students and professionals "to see' the environment "visually" around us. Reading these books and articles has been positively overwhelming while writing this book. Without these scholarss wealth of knowledge and the author's own lifelong drawing and teaching experience, this book would not have been possible.

6.2
Drawing of a memory,
by the author, 2008

We are now entering the third decade of the twenty-first century, where design teachers are required to teach visual literacy more and more with digital tools instead of analog tools like hand sketching. We also now have the additional digital recording tools of tablets or smart phones for hand drawing, for recording sound and movement, and for video to animate observations and new ideas. We also understand the necessity of designing more inclusively for everyone: the wheelchair or mobility device user, the blind or visually impaired, and the deaf or hard of hearing. This, however, also means teaching more inclusive design thinking from the outset of a design problem, in the design studio, and using what this book has sought to coin as "multisensorial literacy". In the above books written by designers and design scholars, the author noticed that only a few specifically suggest including all the senses in the design process. They are first and foremost Juhani Pallasmaa, a pioneer in the field of architecture and the senses, Catherine Dee, and Janet Swailes. There is also the pioneering book on all the main senses by Diane Ackerman's *A Natural History of the Senses*, and more recently Victoria Henshaw's *Urban Smellscapes, Understanding and Designing City Smell Environments*, a fundamental book on smell in environmental design. Ellen Lupton and Andrea Lipps' book *The Senses: Design beyond Vision*, addresses especially the other four main senses apart from sight in design education and practice. Their book has chapters written by scholars and designers with a wealth of inspiring artistic, technical, and useful tools to heighten the attention and necessity of designing multisensorially. Finally, in 2015, *Soundscape and the Built Environment* by Jian Kang and Brigitte Schulte-Fortkamp, which is a compilation of current soundscape research in relation to the built environment by scholars and designers. All these books are fundamental resources to understand the senses with examples of how to experience them and use that experience to create designs. But what was missing until now are pedagogical design exercises to gradually practice using the senses individually, first to observe and record them in the environment, and then to synthesize them for the analysis and design process.

This book provides a guide for "seeing" the world with all five senses. It also provides a theoretical and practical framework and exercises to learn how to observe (see), record, explore, analyze, and include (synthesize) all the main five senses in design. The book acknowledges digital and analog methods and provides students examples from a seminar given in fall 2018 and 2020 called "Seeing Environment at the University of British Columbia. It is suggested that visual literacy and "multisensorial literacy" be practiced throughout the whole first professional design degree in any design field, be it architecture, landscape architecture, urban design, or industrial design. Intentionally, the book is not focusing only on architecture, landscape architecture, urban design, or industrial design, as the author feels that as a designer, one needs to train "seeing" at all environmental scales, because design problems are interconnected.

Further research will be needed in the future to clarify what kinds of exercises are useful to practice multisensorial literacy and their effectiveness. This book does not separate the seeing process of the different design professions to avoid unconsciously creating a hierarchy of the senses and falling into the same trap as in the Renaissance, where sight was preeminent. All senses are important in the design process.

Glossary

analytical sketching
A recording of what cannot be immediately seen.

design analysis
The systematic decision-making process of developing a design; including all information of the design problem in its environmental context, planning, and communications.

environmental experience
Gathering knowledge through the physical experience and observation of the environment.

framework
A visual structure that helps organize the information and ideas of a design problem more effectively.

ideation process
Ideation is idea generation. Big visions are generated through drawings and models, casting a wide net in terms of concept and outcome.

mapping
There are two kinds of mapping: cartographic maps and mind maps for visualizing and analyzing processes, sequences and change through different layers of information. The layering tool is used for analysis and presentation purposes.

metaphor
Metaphor derives from the Greek word metaphora, to "carry over." One kind of object or idea is used in place of another, to suggest a similarity between them or an object, activity, or idea treated as a metaphor.

multisensorial literacy
The ability to understand, analyze, interpret, and make meaning of a space by engaging and using the five senses.

observation of the environment
Environmental observations are key pieces of information that, put together, help build understanding of the environmental context in which the design problem is placed.

olfaction
Olfaction is the sense of smell. Special sensory receptor (cells) called sensory neurons in the nasal cavity connect directly to the brain. Each sensory neuron has one odour receptor. Microscopic molecules released by substances around us—a rose or a forest—stimulate these receptors. Once the neurons detect the molecules, they send messages to the brain, which identifies the smell. There are more smells in the environment than there are receptors, and any given molecule may stimulate a combination of receptors, creating a unique representation in the brain. These representations are registered by the brain as a particular smell.

olfactory
The olfactory system, or sense of smell, is the sensory system used for smelling.

orthographic drawing
A drawing that represents a three-dimensional object using several two-dimensional views of the object, this includes plan, section, and elevation.

perception
Perception refers to the way sensory information is organized, interpreted, and consciously experienced in the environment.

perspective
A three-dimensional representation of the world in a two-dimensional drawing or digital image.

photography
The term photography is derived from Greek words *photos*, which means light, and *graphe*, which means to write—resulting in the direct translation "writing of light". The term *graphe* can also be interpreted as a tool or instrument of recording.

recording
The documentation of the environmental experience through analog (hand drawing), digital (video, sound, photography) images, and body recordings such as memories, emotions, and experiences.

referential sketching
Referential or representational sketching records what can be seen and experienced immediately in front of our eyes.

representation
Representation in this book refers to static visual images drawn by hand or computer and animated images on the computer.

seeing
Seeing does not mean seeing the environment with the eyes alone. It is an overarching term to describe the use of the five senses including: touch, taste, sound and smell.

sensation in the environment
A mental process (such as seeing, hearing, tasting, or smelling) resulting from the immediate external stimulation of a sense organ often as distinguished from a conscious awareness of the sensory process.

senses
The physical abilities of sight, smell, hearing, touch, and taste.

sensorial in design
Sensorial is a less common word for sensory. Sensory information isn't limited to the traditional five senses: sight, smell, taste, touch, and sound. There are many more, however this book focuses only on the five main senses.

sight
Visual sense or the faculty or power of seeing.

site immersion
Site immersion is physical engagement with a site, best by walking, to allow for a multisensorial observation with sound, smell, touch, taste, and sight, and recording of its existing conditions.

synthesis in design
The process of combining design ideas into a design proposal. It is an activity that is done at the end of the creative inquiry. This process leads to creation of a coherent new design.

visual acuity
Studying the environment precisely with your eyes.

vision in design
The personal position in the design synthesis process resulting in a design proposal.

visual literacy
The ability to interpret, negotiate, and make meaning from information presented in the form of an image, extending the meaning of literacy, which commonly signifies interpretation of a written or printed text.

visual thinking
An analytical observation and design process through "looking," which can be learned through practice of observing and recording through sketching, photography or video seeking, and studying patterns in the environment.

Index

accessibility 22, 214
Ackerman, Diane 180, 181, 182, 188, 192, 232
album art exercise *177, 178*
Alto, Alvar 144, 204
analytical sketching 104, *105*, 106, 121–130, 233; above/below ground exercise 127–130, *127, 129, 130*; mapping exercise 123–126, *123, 125, 126*; recommended reading on 15, 204
annotated sketches 9, 14, 30
architecture 8, 108, 166, 168, 232; indigenous 144; and smell 181; and taste 194
audio recording **38**, 184
AutoCAD 10, 15
axonometric drawing **38**, 45, 108

beef platter, analysis of *199–200*
Behnke, Jonathan 213
Benjamin, Walter 134, 205
Bennett, Wayne 6
Berger, John 6, 205, 230
Biddulph, M. 4
birdsong 8, 36
blind people see visually impaired people
blindfolds 62, 146, 148, 154, 167, 218
block diagrams 31
bodily experience 4, 6, 8, 146, 166, 167, 212
body space, tactile 155–158, *155, 157–158*
book exchanges *137–138*
Boston (US) 87–88
Bourbonne, A. 16
brain 10, 12, *19*, 23
Brumberger, E.R. 10

Campbell, Marissa 109, 113–114, 125, 127, 145, 157–158, 173, 197–198, 215
Canada 7, 62, 133, see also Vancouver
Cen, Vicky *139–140, 161–162*
Cerwén, Gunnar 168
chair, sensorial design of *47–48*
Chen, Mingjia *151–152*
Chicago (US) 95–96
China 63–66, *64, 65, 66*

Ching, Francis D.K. 203, 204, 228
Cleveland (US) 97–98
collage/photomontage 9, 14, **38**, 45, 184
context, environmental 12, 14, 22, 36
Copeland, L. 167
COVID 19 pandemic 8, 217
Craig, Doug *174*, 218
Crowe, Norman 9, 104, 108, 122, 204, 230
Crown Sky Garden (US) 95–96
cultural experiences see historic/cultural experiences

dance **38**, *163*, 164, 167
Darowski, Jacob *171–172, 189–190, 201*
deaf people 36
Dee, Catherine 9, 15, 146, 204, 230, 232
Delhi (India) 91–92
design education 212–222, 230–232; and accessible/inclusive design 214; and drawing 212–216, 217–220; drawing neglected in 9–10; and fear of failure 217–220; and learning through repetition 214; and multisensorial literacy 212; and multisensorial perception 8, 218; and multisensorial teaching checklist 221–222; online 217, 220; and playfulness/experimentation 220; and reading space 9; and site immersion 8, 12, 220; and skill training 214–216; and syllabus design 216–217; and visual literacy books 230 design ideas 14, 15, 31, 32, 214 design phase 12, 20 design phases/process 27–34; final design 27, 34, *34*; ideation 12, 27, 33, *33*, 45; recording see recording; site analysis see site analysis; site immersion see site immersion; synthesis 27, 31, 32, *32*
design programs 9, 32
design proposals 33, 34
Diagonal Records 167
diagrams 9, 14, 31, 32, 34, 36, 45; analytical 38

digital design tools 4, 9, 14, 15, 30, 36, 170, 214; and design education 214, 218, 232; and hand drawing, compared 10–12, *11*, 106; photography 132
digital devices 146, *see also* smart phones; tablets
digital modelling 31, 34, **38**
drawing 4, 10, 12, 15, 106, 212–216; axonometric **38**, 45, 108; elevation 31, 45, 108; and fear of failure 217–220; gestural *5*; hand/digital, compared 10–12, *11*, 15, 106; and ideation 33, *33*; and learning through repetition 214; neglected in design schools 9–10, 217–218; orthographic 32, 108, 234; as personal response 10; perspective 31, **38**, 45, 108, 234; recommended reading on 203; and site analysis 31; and tactile boards *153*, *154*; tools 32, *see also* diagrams; sketching; visual notes
Drazil, David 214, 220
drinking object, design of *201*, *202*
drones **38**, 134

echoes 167
ecological aspects 8, 36, 62, 132
Eins + Alles – Experience Field of the Senses (Germany) 93–94
elevation drawing 31, 45, 108
Elizabeth & Nona Evans Restorative Garden (US) 97
emotions 6, 24, 184
exploded view 31

failure, fear of 217–220
Featherstone, Guy 167
fence, sensorial design of 49–50
Fender, Josh *159*
field sketching *see* sketching
fieldwork 8
Fin Garden (Iran) 67–70, *68*, *69*, *70*
fire alarms 36
flavour 26, 167, 192–194, *see also* taste
Flores, M. 214, 220
food 42, 192–200, *197–198*; architecture as 194; fake *193*, *194*, 202; and flavour *see* flavour; and smell 94, 182; and taste rave exercise 195–200, *195*, *197–198*, *199–200*
fountains 69, 75, 76, *76*, 77, *77*, 78, *78*, 80, 85, 88, 92, 96

Gagnon-Creeley, Michelle *131*, *133*, *141*, *163*
Gao, Kemeng 169, 185–186
Garden of Five Senses (India) 91–92
gardens *see* parks/gardens
gazebos 62
Germany 93–94, *107*
gestural drawings 5
Google Maps 10
Gram, Yette *137–138*
Grand Tour 108
grass 88, 98, 146; olfactory experience of 182, *183*
Graves, Michael 108, 204

Habjanic, Rozman/Habjanic, Gasper 220
hand use exercise 147–152, *147*, *149–150*, *151–152*
Hart, Samantha *183*
Have, R. 32
healing *see* restorative gardens
hearing *see* sound
Henshaw, Victoria 62, 182, 188, 206, 232
Hidcote Manor Garden (Chipping Campden, UK) 79–82, *80*, *81*, *82*
historic/cultural experiences 62, 63, 67, 71, 75, 134
holistic approach 6, 8, 29
Holl, Steven 144
Humble Administrator's Garden (China) 63–66, *64*, *65*, *66*
Hutchinson, Edward 10, 15, 203, 230

ideation process 12, 20, 27, 33, *33*, 45, 220, 233
inclusive design 214, 232
India 91–92
industrial design 36, 192
initial design vision 20, 31
Instagram 132, 203, 220

Japan 26, 36, 71–74, 89–90, 181
jazz album covers 167, *177*, *178*

Jenkins, Eric 9, 15, 104, 108, 122, 203, 230
Johnston, Lawrence 79

Kang, Jian 232
Katsura Imperial Villa Gardens (Japan) 71–74
Kessler, Berend *135, 199–200*
Kükelhaus, Hugo 93
Kyoto (Japan) 71–74

Landau, Steven 144, 154
landscape architecture 8, 9, 34, 108, 168, 192; recommended reading on 15; teaching 212, 232
Laseau, Paul 9, 104, 108, 122, 204, 230
Latour, Bruno 12
Lipps, Andrea *57*, 180, 182, 194, 202, 206, 232
Lobmueller, Fabian *162*
Lupton, Ellen *57*, 146, 166, 167, 202, 206, 232

McLean, Kate 62, 182, 188
maps/mapping 30, 31, 32, 36, **38**, 134, 233; exercise in 123–126, *123, 125, 126*; and smells 62, 182, 184
material collection **38**
materiality 22, 53, 56, *76, 77*, 146
May, John 10, 12
medical students 212
memory 6, 20, 24, 25, 26, 43–44; drawing *7, 231*; and smell 180, 184
mindfulness 6, 8, 20, 24, 39
models 9, **38**
modernism 144
Monumental Garden of Valsanzibio (Italy) 75–78, *76, 77, 78*
Mooney, Patrick 181
Moore, K. 9
movement exercise 159–162, *159, 161, 162*
multisensorial diagnostics 212
multisensorial literacy 4, 20–24, 108, 232, 233; and initial design vision 20, 31; and multisensorial perception, compared 14; and site immersion *see* site immersion; teaching 212, 214; and textured surfaces 22; and uses of senses 20
multisensorial observation exercises 14, 36
multisensorial perception 6, *13*, 36, 218; and drawing 12, 214; drawing/visualization tools 37, **38**; and multisensorial literacy, compared 14; and site immersion 8, 12
multisensorial recording 30
multisensorial teaching check list 221–222
Murcutt, Glen 144
music **38**, 65, 166, 167, *177, 178*

New York City (US) *169*, 185–186
Nietzsche, Friedrich 166
Northcut, K.M. 10

object design 194, *201*, 202
oblique view 31
observation 23, 24, *41–42, 43–44*, 106, 154, 233; and design education 216, 217, 220
ofuro bathtubs 181
Oizumi Ryokuchi Park (Japan) 89–90
Okanagan Valley (Canada) 7
olfaction *see* smell
one-point perspective 144
online teaching 217, 220
orange, experience of eating *197–198*
orthographic drawings 32, 108, 234
Osaka (Japan) 89–90

Pallasmaa, Juhani 4, 6, 8, 15, 24, 144, 167, 168, 180, 181, 230, 232
parks/gardens *21–22*, 22, 36, **40**, 62–100, 167; Crown Sky Garden (US) 95–96; Eins + Alles - Experience Field of the Senses (Germany) 93–94; Elizabeth & Nona Evans Restorative Garden (US) 97; Fin Garden (Iran) 67–70, *68, 69, 70*; Garden of Five Senses (India) 91–92; Hidcote Manor Garden (Chipping Campden, UK) 79–82, *80, 81, 82*; Humble Administrator's Garden (China) 63–66, *64, 65, 66*; Katsura Imperial Villa Gardens (Japan) 71–74; Monumental Garden of Valsanzibio (Italy) 75–78, *76, 77, 78*; Oizumi Ryokuchi Park (Japan) 89–90; restorative 36, 95, 97; and synthesizing checklist 53–56; Villandry Gardens (France) 83–86,

84, 85, 86; water features in *see* water features; William E. Carter School Sensory Gardens (US) 87–88

participatory research 62, 182
paths, texture/materiality of 22, 56, 76, 77
pavilions 62
perception 6, 8, 12, 14, 23, 232; and interaction of senses 41–42, 43–44; and observation 23, 24; recommended reading on 15
performance 14
pergolas 62
perspective drawing 31, **38**, 45, 108, 234
photography 8, 30, 36, **38**, 45, 131–142, 234; annotated 136, 142; digital 132; limitations of 10; and passage of time 132, 141–142, *141*; recommended reading on 205; as visual thinking 132, 134, 135–140, *135, 137–138, 139–140*
photomontage *see* collage/photomontage
Pierre, Kathryn *118, 119, 126, 195*
plan view 31, **38**, 45, 108, 124
plants 79, 87, 124; and sight 55, 56, 88, 90, 124, 127, 128, 136; and smell 53, 56, 82, 98, 181; and sound 167; and touch 53, 56, 80, 90, 98, 146; *see also* grass; trees
podcasts 14
Puente, Valia *147*

Ratzlaff, Jenna *115, 130, 155*
recording 14, 27, 30, *30*, 37–38, **38**, 234; and design education 212, 214, 216, 217, 218, 220; and handheld digital devices 36; *see also specific recording tools*
referential sketching 9, 104, *105*, 106–120, 234; adding dimension exercise 115–120, *115, 117, 118, 119, 120*; line-drawing exercise 109–114, *109, 111, 112, 113–114*; recommended reading on 203
Reid, Jennifer *149–150*
Renaissance 4, 144, 181
restorative gardens 36, 95, 97
Ruskin, John 194

Sachs, Oliver 166

scale 9, 20, 37, 45, 232
Schafer, Raymond Murray 62, 168
Schulte-Fortkamp, Brigitte 232
seashells *145*
section view 31, **38**, 45, 108
seeing 4–10, 234; and drawing 12; history of 4; importance for designers of 8; as multisensorial 6, 8; and perception 6; and pre-eminence of sight 4, 9
senses 4–6, 15, 20, 25–26, 234; and brain 23; hierarchy of 4, 9, 14, 144, 181; interconnectedness/interaction of 35, 39, **40**, *41–42, 43–44,* 167; interpretation methods for 36; prioritizing importance of, checklist for 46–56; and site immersion 8; *see also specific senses*
sensewalks 62; *see also under* smell; sound; taste; touch
sensorial design synthesizing list 45–56
Shepard, Gordon M. 192
shoelace, sound of *175*
sight 103–142, 235; and brain 12, 23, 25; and design context 36; in interaction with other senses *35,* **40**, *41–42, 43–44,* 106; and one-point perspective 144; pre-eminence of 4, 9, 14, 144, 181, 212; and recording tools **38**; and seeing, compared 6
site analysis 10, 15, 27, 29, 31, *31,* 32, 36, 45
site immersion 10, 15, 20, 22, 235; and design education 8, 12, 220; as design phase 27, 28, 29, *29*; and interaction of senses **40**; multiple repetitions of 29; and recording 30
sketching 9–10, 14, 15, 30, 36, 104–122; analytical *see* analytical sketching; annotated 9, 14; benefits of 12; and design education 214–216, 217–218; hand/digital, compared 10–12, *11,* 106, 214; referential *see* referential sketching
skill training 214–216
skin 25, 57, 144, 146, 214; and sound 166
smart phones 36, 134, 146
smell 6, 8, 9, 14, 26, 179–190, 216; and brain 23; cultural aspects of 181, 182; describing 182, 188;

ephemeral/personal nature of 180; and fire alarms 36; and flavour 26, 167, 192–194; on garden sensewalks 66, 70, 74, 78, 82, 86, 88, 90, 92, 94; in interaction with other senses 35, **40**, 41–42, 43–44; and memory/imagination 180, 181, 184; overlooked in design 180, 181–182; recommended reading on 206, 232; recording tools for **38**; smell notes exercise 183–186, *183, 185–186*; and taste 192; in urban environment 62, 181

smell maps 62, 182, 187–190, *187, 188–189*
smell notes exercise 183–186, *183, 185–186*
smellwalks 62, 182, 188
Sontag, Susan 132, 205, 230
sound 8, 9, 14, 26, 165–178; album art exercise *177, 178*; and blindfolding 62; and brain 12, *23*; and deaf people 36; in garden sensewalks 62, 65, 69, 73, 77, 81, 85, 88, 90, 92, 94, 96; in interaction with other senses 35, **40**, 41–42, 43–44; and listening skills 168, 206; music **38**, 65, 166, 167, *177, 178*; recommended reading on 205–206; recording 30, **38**, 156, 170, 176, 184, 216; and space 167; and synesthesia 167; tuning in exercise 169–174, *169, 171–172, 173, 174*; and urban environment 166, 168, 176; wind play exercise *175, 176*
soundscapes/soundwalks 168, 170
Suzhou (China) 63–66, *64, 65, 66*
Swailes, Janet 8, 15, 204, 214, 230, 232
synesthesia 167
synthesis (design phase) 27, 31, 32, 235; checklist for 45–56
synthesis (perception) 39, *41–42, 43–44*

tablets (digital tool) 14, 36, 106, 136, 217, 232
tactile body space exercise 155–158, *155, 157–158*
tactile drawing boards *153, 154*
taste 6, 9, 14, 26, 191–202, 216; and brain 23, 192; and colour 194; and fake food *193, 194*, 202; on garden sensewalks 74, 82, 86, 88, 90, 92, 94; importance of 192; in interaction with other senses 35, **40**, 41–42, 43–44; as multisensorial experience 192, 194; and object design 194, 201, 202; recommended reading on 206; recording tools for 38, *see also* flavour
taste rave exercise 195–200, *195, 197–198, 199–200*
temperature 26, 30
text 14, 30, **38**, 216
3D modelling 34, 37, 45
Tilley, Christopher 6
touch 4, 6, 14, 25, 143–164; and blindfolding 146, 148, 154; and brain 12, *23*; dancing/figure skating exercise 64, *163*; on garden sensewalks 64, 68, 72, 76, 80, 84, 88, 90, 92, 94, 96; hand use exercise 147–152, *147, 149–150, 151–152*; importance of 144, 146; in interaction with other senses 35, **40**, 41–42, 43–44; movement exercise 159–162, *159, 161, 162*; recording tools for **38**; tactile body space exercise 155–158, *155, 157–158*; tactile drawing board exercise *153, 154*; textured surfaces 22, 56, *157–158*
trees 70, 92, 94, 124, 128, 167
Treib, Marc 10, 15, 230
Tufte, Edward 57, 124
tuning in exercise 169–174, *169, 171–172, 173, 174*
typing, sound of *173*

United States (US) 87–88, 95–96, *97–98, 185–186*
urban environment 8, 15, 232; smells in 62, 181, 182; sounds in 167, 168, 176

van den Toorn, M. 32
Vancouver (Canada) 62, *123, 130, 171–172, 187, 189–190,* 219
Verona (Italy) 194
video 8, 14, 36, **38**, 45, 216; 3D 34
Villandry Gardens (France) 83–86, *84, 85, 86*

vision *see* sight
visual acuity 9, 104, 108, 116, 235
visual literacy 4, 9, 12, 14, 104, 108, 232, 235; reading on 230
visual notes 8, 9, 15, 36, **38**
visual perception 194
visual sense *see* seeing
visual thinking 132, 134, 135–140, *135, 137–138, 139–140*, 212, 235
visually impaired people 49, 89, 154, 214, 232
Vogelzang, Marije 202

wall, partitioning, sensorial design of 51–52
Wansink, Brian 194
water features 68, 69, 80, 81, 83, 84, 85, 88; waterfalls *72, 72, 73, 73*, see *also* fountains
Wenwen Zhuang *112, 120, 129, 175*
Westerkamp, Hildegard 62, 170, 176, 182, 205–206
wheelchairs 22, 214, 232
Whiston Spirn, Anne 132, 134, 205, 212, 230
wildlife 8, 36, 65, 81
William E. Carter School Sensory Gardens (US) 87–88
wind, sound of *175*, 176
Wright, Frank Lloyd 144, 204

Yaying Zhou *111, 117*
YouTube 99, 132, 205, 220

Zumthor, Peter 144